The Little Alamo

The Real Life Story of Bradford's Bandits at Dong Ha Air Base, Vietnam
1965-1966

The Little Alamo

The Real Life Story of Bradford's Bandits at Dong Ha Air Base, Vietnam
1965-1966

William D. Bland

Foreword by Carl L. Bradford
Master Sergeant, USAF (Ret.)

Word Association Publishers
205 Fifth Avenue
Tarentum, Pennsylvania 15084

ISBN 10: 1-59571-124-4
ISBN 13: 978-1-59571-124-3
Library of Congress Control Number: 2006923517

Word Association Publishers
205 Fifth Avenue,
Tarentum, Pennsylvania 15084
www.wordassociation.com
1-800-827-7903

Sarge

This book is a tribute to Master Sergeant Carl L. Bradford (U.S. Air Force, Retired) and his troops, defenders of Dong Ha Air Base, Republic of Vietnam, 1965-1966. Sergeant Bradford was our leader and "Top Cop" at Dong Ha. Forty years later, we are still his Bandits. Respect is earned, not given by rank or position; however, Sergeant Bradford was a bona fide leader of men. Today, we could call him Carl or Brad, but we still call him Sarge.

Tech. Sergeant Bradford, Dong Ha, 1966

Master Sergeant Bradford's military awards include Air Force Commendation Medal w/1 OLC, Air Force Outstanding Unit Award with V device and 1/ BSS, Air Force Good Conduct Medal w/2 OLCs, National Defense Service Medal w/1 BSS, Armed Forces Expeditionary Medal, U.S. Vietnam Service Medal with/1 BSS, Air Force Longevity Service Award Ribbon w/4 OLCs, Air Force Small Arms Expert Marksmanship Ribbon, and Vietnam Campaign Medal.

Bradford's Bandits

The Original Eleven

Carl L. Bradford,

Jack J. Case, Edward F. Cheri, Robert M. Stemock,

David L. Black, Sam "Dino" Baldon, John A. "Bert" Bertolet,

William D. Bland, David M. Green, Joseph L. Lee,

and James H. Schneider

Honorary Bandits

William "Doc" Grover and Terry G. Sandman

Acknowledgements

I served as an Air Policeman in the United States Air Force from 1963 to 1967, including a tour of duty in Vietnam (1965-1966). It was during my Vietnam service that I met ten of the finest men that I have ever had the privilege to be associated with, before or after. This story is about a small, elite group of U.S. Air Force combat policemen from the 6250th Air Police Squadron, Tan Son Nhut Air Base, Republic of Vietnam, who volunteered for reassignment to Dong Ha. At the time, we knew very little about Dong Ha except that it was located near the DMZ (Demilitarized Zone) and that it was a hot area where firefights occurred nightly. We were led by TSgt. Carl Bradford and acquired the nickname "Bradford's Bandits" for our exploits en route to Dong Ha via Da Nang Air Base. This book is an outgrowth of the war stories told by the Bandits following our first reunion in 2002 and afterwards. I relied heavily on these stories in writing this book. Individually, some of us recall certain circumstances vividly, while other events have somewhat faded from memory, simply by the passage of time. Collectively, we have been able to reconstruct a part of the history at Dong Ha that portrays our part in the war. The Bandit story could not have been written by one person alone, it was a collaborative effort. This is our story—the Bandit story. It is also the story, in part, of William "Doc" Grover, our medic at Dong Ha, and Terry Sandman, an Air Policeman who served at Dong Ha after the Bandits left. I want to thank all the Bandits for their contributions to this book. It seemed only fitting that the leader of the Bandits, Carl Bradford, should write the Foreword in any book about the Bandits. I wish especially to acknowledge Sam Baldon, John Bertolet, David Black, Jack Case, Ed Cheri, Doc Grover, David Green, Joe Lee, Terry Sandman, Jim Schneider, and Bob Stemock for their roles in helping me write this book.

—William D. Bland

Foreword[1]

In reviewing my life and military career in the U.S. Air Force, like most people, I have had my share of good times and some bad. However, as I look back, the period of my life spent at a little place called Dong Ha during the Vietnam War was one of my most memorable experiences. I was fortunate to be placed in charge of a great group of airmen, all volunteers who agreed to go with me to a little outpost near the DMZ. It was a dangerous assignment and these men were my responsibility. They were my troops and I was determined to do the best job I could to bring them all home safely. It was an honor for me to have served with such courageous men. And no one was more surprised than me that thirty-six years later I would see them all again.

I was a thirty-three year old Tech Sergeant in 1965 and the airmen under my command were mostly twenty year olds. They didn't know, nor would I have told them at the time, how much I missed my wife and family and wanted so much to be back home. But we had a job to do and I can say without reservation that these young men did everything I asked them to do and more. No leader could have ever asked for a more professional group than these ten young airmen.

Sometime in November 1965, a notice was posted on the Bulletin Board at the APO (Air Police Office). It called for one TSgt. and ten Air Policemen to volunteer for an assignment up North. I volunteered and got the job. The First Sergeant told me I could pick anyone on the list. I picked the first ten names on the list. The First Sergeant cut the orders and I met with the ten Air Policemen sometime in December. I called the roll off the orders and told them what I knew about where we were going, which was very little.

In mid December 1965, I received a message to report to Colonel Black in the 2nd Air Division Headquarters, in the Cholon district of Saigon. I reported as directed and was briefed

[1] Abridged version of "A Message to My Troops," by Carl L. Bradford, MSgt. (Ret.), originally published in *Tiger Flight, 13* (3), 2004, pp. 37–41. Used with permission.

by Col. Black about our mission to Dong Ha, near the DMZ. Our unit designation was Detachment 1, 620th Tactical Control Squadron. The headquarters for this outfit was on top of Monkey Mountain near Da Nang AB.

Col. Black was the Director of all Air Police units in South Vietnam and was on General Moore's (2nd Air Division Commander) staff. The Colonel and I had a good talk about the mission to Dong Ha and then he asked me if I was ready to go? I said, "Yes sir, I am." During the meeting, Col. Black told me if I had any problems with the radar unit about security operations to give him a call and he would take care of it. As it turned out, Major Cummings, the radar site commander, was a good officer and he never interfered with the way I ran things at Dong Ha.

After the meeting with the Colonel, I briefed the troops about what I knew and told to them to get ready for our trip up to Dong Ha. I also asked them to use their whiskey rations and buy as much liquor as they could. I had been in the service long enough to know that we wouldn't be given all that we needed to get the job done. With those bottles of whiskey we could do some trading with the Marines at Da Nang to get the things we needed.

We were scheduled to leave Tan Son Nhut on December 26 or December 27, 1965. Before we left, I took time out to write my wife and children. I missed them so very much, but I couldn't let my emotions show, because I was the leader. I called the roll and prepared to board the C-123 for our first leg to Da Nang Air Base. At Da Nang, we turned in our military records, because where we were going was a remote outpost. We spent two nights at Da Nang. While we were waiting to board our plane to take us to Dong Ha, I noticed the troops going over to a C-130 and walking back to our plane. They made a couple of trips, so I walked over to the C-130 and asked what they were doing? They said, "Nothing Sarge," and I told them that they looked like a bunch of damned Bandits. They said, "Yeah Sarge, we're your Bandits." And that is the way Bradford's Bandits got started and good Bandits they were. However, it got me to thinking, what else have these guys been up to?

Other than a couple of meetings before leaving for Dong Ha that was all the contact I had had with these troops. They didn't know me and I didn't know them. However, the incident on the flight line at Da Nang had broken the ice; they had accepted me as their leader and they were my "Bandits." As the plane rolled down the runway, I was beginning to feel better already about the airmen I had selected for this assignment.

Dong Ha was about eighty miles north of Da Nang. We sat down on the dirt runway and were briefly greeted by the troops we were replacing. We hardly had any time to talk to the TDY Air Policemen because they were leaving on the same plane that had just brought us in. The pilot was in a real hurry too. As I would learn later, planes didn't spend much time on the ground at Dong Ha; just enough time to drop off troops or supplies and then get out of there as quickly as they could.

I surveyed the camp, and assigned my troops to their positions along the perimeter. I assigned A1C Stemock to the Command Post. He was in charge of communications. I was fortunate to have three really top-notched senior airmen to help me. A1Cs Case and Stemock had completed Air Commando training and A1C Cheri was a career Air Policeman. A2Cs Baldon, Bertolet, Black, Bland, Green, Lee, and Schneider were seasoned security troops, all had at least two or more years in the service before coming to Vietnam, and they all had been in-country for several months.

We stowed our gear in a tent and then hit the berm. The berm was not much more than a few sandbag bunkers with dirt piled up around them. I don't remember if the 50 cals. were set up that first night, but within a couple of days we had placed 50 cal. machine guns on three corners of the compound. The 50 cals. were positioned so that maximum firepower would cover the east, south, and southwest perimeters. That was where any VC threat was most likely to come from. A minefield and several strands of concertina wire protected the east and south berm. We really didn't have enough troops to man the entire perimeter. We were spread thin, but we had three sides of the camp covered. The north wall faced the ARVN (South Vietnamese soldiers) compound, however I didn't feel comfortable leaving it unmanned.

It was our first night at Dong Ha. My troops were locked and loaded and on their posts before dark. I was in the Command Post part of the time, but I also patrolled behind the bunkers. I carried a shotgun rather than a M-16. I felt that in close-in quarters a shotgun would be more effective. I checked on the troops several times during the night to see how they were doing. They were squared away and alert for action. I was certain by then that I had picked ten good troops that could handle the job.

From that day onward, they would be in their positions, with weapons at the ready from dusk to dawn. We didn't have formal guardmounts before going out on post. The troops knew what I expected of them and I did not have to tell them what to do. They knew their job and I didn't have to worry about them doing it. I suppose that we all felt that we were as strong as the weakest link and no one was going to let the others down. Our very lives depended on everybody doing their job. And these troops were not afraid to get their hands dirty. When they were not on post, they were building sandbag bunkers and doing whatever else that needed to be done.

On January 8, 1966, Dong Ha Air Base was attacked with mortars and small arms fire, but I was not there. I think that was when I had gone to Tan Son Nhut to pick up some M-60 machine guns. I returned with the guns, 7.62 rounds for the M-60s, additional 2.23 rounds for the M-16s, and extra ammo for the 50 cals., slap flares, and other equipment. When I got back, I took the troops out to test fire the M-60s and taught them how to fire the M-60 so as not to burn up the barrel. They were all expert rifle marksmen and familiar with weapons so they learned quickly.

My Bandits had already been in their first firefight and I was tremendously proud of the way they had handled themselves— they were now veteran combat troops. And with the M-60s added to the 50 cal. positions, every Air Police bunker was a machine gun post.

On February 4, 1966, around 2200 hours, mortars came in from two directions. I don't know how many rounds we received but it was pretty heavy. The war had come our way again, however we were ready for them. A1C Bob Stemock got a pretty good fix on their positions and was able to direct out-going fire. Two Air Force F-4 pilots came in and dropped napalm on VC (Viet Cong) positions about five miles north of our site.

We had no casualties or major damage, but a click higher and Major Cummings might have been killed. One round landed just outside his quarters. A number of tents had holes in them, a meat-locker was destroyed and the chow hall was slightly damaged, and I believe the latrine took a hit.

After that second major mortar attack, Dong Ha Air Base was being referred to as the "Little Alamo." Soon after that attack, we received four more air policemen to help us defend the site. I don't remember all their names, but one was A2C Haney.

My time at Dong Ha was growing short and soon I would be leaving the Bandits, Doc, Major Cummings, and the other troops of the 620th. These were good men; courageous, and men of character. However, even though I dreaded leaving my Bandits, I was anxious to see my wife and children. By this point I was exhausted, down to 150 pounds compared with 175 pounds when I had left home.

My replacement, SSgt. Hester arrived at Dong Ha about the middle of March 1966. We had a change of command ceremony in which I was able to stand tall for my troops at my last guardmount with them. I will never forget the going away party my Bandits gave me. Then, on March 27, 1966, Major Cummings drove me to the runway and all the Bandits were present to see me off. I hadn't cried since I left my wife and children. However, I had to bite my lip so that my troops wouldn't see me cry. We said our goodbyes and I was about to board the aircraft when all of a sudden my troops picked me up on their shoulders and put me in the plane. I stood at the door for a moment and looked at my Bandits for the last time. I wouldn't see them again until thirty-six years later when we all got together for a reunion in Myrtle Beach, SC.

I never forgot my Bandits. My time with these young men had a profound effect on my life from that time to the present. We were close as brothers, and in fact we are brothers. Each one is special to me and I still love my Bandits.

I retired from the Air Force on December 4, 1972. I had served with a lot of good men in my twenty year plus career, but none more courageous or as dedicated as these ten young air policemen. If I were to ever go back into battle, these are the men I would choose to be with me. During our brief time together at Dong Ha in 1965-1966, they earned my trust and respect. And the bond we shared is still with us today.

— Carl L. Bradford
Master Sergeant, USAF (Ret.)

Contents

Tan Son Nhut

The story of Bradford's Bandits begins at Tan Son Nhut Air Base near Saigon, South Vietnam in 1965. In November, the commander of the 6250th Air Police Squadron placed a message on the bulletin board asking for volunteers to go to a place no one had heard of before. It was remote site up North near the DMZ called Dong Ha. We were told that it would be dangerous, that firefights were a nightly occurrence. Because of the remote location, if we were attacked by a large enemy force, there would be no one to help us. Though we all volunteered for this assignment, most of us did not know one another at Tan Son Nhut. Once we learned who was going to Dong Ha, we met at the Airman's Club and got to know each other. We all had one thing in common; we all had volunteered to leave the relative luxury and security of TSN to go to a remote outpost near the DMZ.[1] We were a close-knit group from the very beginning and the bond continued throughout our tour at Dong Ha. Perhaps we felt special because of the small size of our unit and the fact that we were going into harm's way.

All of us had voluntarily joined the Air Force and each had his own reason, perhaps, for doing so. Some had joined for patriotic reasons and some may have chosen to enlist to avoid being drafted into the Army. John Bertolet gave the following reasons:

> I am an American and believe that what we did in Vietnam to try stop communism was the right thing to do at the time. I had enlisted in the Air Force and had volunteered to go to Vietnam. I shaped up thanks to the military, grew up a great deal, and became a bit more of a man while I was in the service.[2]

---

[1] Bland, William D. "Bradford's Bandits: A Tribute to Carl Bradford, MSgt. (Ret.) and His Defenders of Dong Ha Air Base, Vietnam, 1965-1966." *Tiger Flight, 11* (6), 2002, pp. 37-41.

[2] Bertolet, John A. "Letters Home from Vietnam." *Tiger Flight, 13* (4), 2004, pp. 37-42.

Dave Green cited more practical reasons for joining the Air Force:

> Men of our generation knew that military service was a preordained fact of life. We were going to serve: how long, when, and which branch was our choice, but the bottom line was at least two years in the U. S. Army. That bottom line would come in an official, white envelope, with the salutation, "Greetings," along with directions and explanations as to why our butts were now U. S. property. The Draft![3]

Most of us had enlisted right after high school in either 1962 or 1963. That was around the time of the Cuban missile crisis and President John F. Kennedy's assassination. Vietnam was just beginning. I recalled seeing some newsreels showing Vietnam villages being attacked by Viet Cong (VC). However, it was not until March 1965 that the first American combat troops landed at Da Nang. Tan Son Nhut Air Base was located in the South, just outside of Saigon. Beginning in April 1965, one by one, the Bandits arrived at this joint military base/civilian airport.

Tech. Sergeant Bradford arrived for duty in Vietnam in early April. He described what it was like in those first few days:

> Vietnam was hot and humid and it took me awhile to get acclimated to the weather. What I remember most was the noise, the constant whop, whop, whop of helicopters twenty-four hours a day, the smell of the morgue where our valiant young soldiers were prepared to go home, and the body bags loaded in tractor trailers, stacked like cordwood on the flight line.[4]

Like his older brothers who had served in WWII, Sergeant Bradford had volunteered for Vietnam. Thirty-nine years later, he said:

---

[3] Personal communication with Dave Green on March 2, 2004.
[4] Bradford, Carl L. "A Message to My Troops: Defenders of Dong Ha Air Base, Republic of Vietnam, 1965-1966." *Tiger Flight, 13* (3), 2004, pp. 37-41.

I don't regret going to Vietnam, but I wish that the outcome of the war had been different. With all the anti-war protests back home, Vietnam veterans did not get a welcome home, as did the troops returning from WWII. I didn't talk about my Vietnam experience, however I knew in my heart that I had done my best and that's all anyone could do.[5]

Saigon was the largest city and the capital of South Vietnam (Republic of Vietnam). Tan Son Nhut Air Base was located just outside of Saigon. Headquarters for the 2nd Air Division (USAF), later redesignated the 7th Air Force (April 1, 1966), was also located in Saigon. It was guarded by air police from the 6250th APS.

We all had volunteered for Vietnam. Most of us had served in combat defense units on SAC (Strategic Air Command) bases guarding nuclear weapons, i.e., Minuteman missiles and B-52 bombers. I was with the 821st Combat Defense Squadron at Ellsworth AFB, South Dakota. One of the things about SAC bases, particularly those with missile wings, were that they were located in isolated areas of the United States, all with very cold climates. During the winter at bases located in Michigan, Missouri, South Dakota, North Dakota, Wyoming, and Montana, it was not uncommon for the wind chill factor to drop below seventy degrees Fahrenheit. As air police, we stood guard duty for eight to twelve hours, regardless of weather. It was the height of the Cold War, both literally and figuratively, and SAC bases were on alert twenty-four hours a day, seven days a week.

I had already spent one winter at Ellsworth AFB, SD. In August 1964, President Lyndon B. Johnson announced the Gulf of Tonkin Resolution. I was on the bomber pad when the call came out for volunteers for Vietnam service.[6] Air police had to go through a very stringent screening process at that time (a situation that soon changed as the build up in Vietnam occurred), involving not only a personal interview with the squadron commander but also with the wing commander.

I was approved to go and received my orders for Vietnam,

[5] *Ibid*, p. 38.
[6] Bland, William D. "The Little Alamo: Dong Ha Air Base, Vietnam, 1965-1966." *Tiger Flight*, 8 (4), 1999, pp. 31-32.

landing at Tan Son Nhut Air Base in July 1965. I was assigned to the 6250th Air Police Squadron. The 6250th was the first air police unit to wear the Blue Beret with the QC patch.[7] The Quan Cahn (QC) were the Vietnamese military police and were feared by the Vietnamese people. The QC patch identified us with the Quan Cahn, which I am not certain was a good thing—but it reinforced our authority with the Vietnamese people.

A2C Bland, 6250th APS, 1965

In early 1965, the 6250th Air Police Squadron was responsible for providing law and order on this large Air Force base. Air Police were the military police of the Air Force. However, in its brief fifty-some year history, the U.S. Air Force has changed the name of its military police several times. First, from Military Police to Air Police in 1948, right after the Air Force separated from the Army Air Force (AAF) in 1947, second from Air Police to Security Police in 1966, and more recently in 1997 to Security Forces. The motto of today's Security Forces is *Defensor Fortis* (Defenders of the Force).

Our main job in Vietnam was air base defense and security. We walked the line along the perimeter, often alone rather than in large units or strike forces. Our job was to spot and engage the

---

[7] *Ibid*, p. 31.

Viet Cong (the enemy) before they could make it to the flight line to destroy fighter aircraft or other valuable resources and personnel.

John Bertolet, Tan Son Nhut, 1965

Sergeant Bradford recalled a powerful memory of an inadvertent meeting he had with two Air Force EOD (Explosive Ordnance Disposal) team members outside the Air Police Operations building at TSN:

> I met an Air Force Captain and TSgt. who were on their way to Bien Hoa Air Base, about 15 miles from TSN. Just a few days later on May 16, 1965, there was a huge explosion at Bein Hoa. Later that day, I learned that a B-57 bomber had dropped a live bomb onto the parking apron, which caused a chain reaction and the explosion of several aircraft. The next day, I went to Bein Hoa and witnessed firsthand the aftermath of the terrible damage that had occurred there. The Captain and TSgt. that I had talked to just days before had been killed trying to defuse the bombs.[8]

---

[8] Bradford, "A Message to My Troops," p. 38.

On December 4, 1965, Viet Cong terrorists bombed a hotel used by U.S. military personnel, killing eight and wounding 137. There were a number of hotel bombings in Saigon during our tour at Tan Son Nhut. John Bertolet commented: "I was assigned hotel guard duty many times. Now, that was a dangerous job. The people came right up to you and you had to be especially careful since it was hard to tell the good guys from the bad guys (Viet Cong).[9]

Air police also guarded Lt. General Joseph H. Moore's quarters in downtown Saigon. Gen. Moore was the 2nd Air Division Commander and later became the 7th Air Force Commander on April 1, 1966.

In the passage below, Dave Green describes one night on post at General Moore's quarters. Apparently, this was before the big buildup of troops at Tan Son Nhut and prior to the activation of the 6250th Air Police Squadron. Dave said:

> Our commander was not an Air Policeman; he was a major, but a nice guy (for a major). I remember once I sat down while on guard duty in the General's Quarters. Now after spending three years in S.A.C. I had perfected the ability of sleeping on watch. I heard the crunch of feet on gravel and knew I was probably busted, so I shouted, "TAKE ONE MORE STEP ASSHOLE AND YOU'RE A DEAD MAN!" "Oh, Geez Green! I thought you were asleep!" "Asleep? Not on a post this important, Major. You better be more careful walking these posts, Sir you could end up dead." "I'll try to do that, thanks Green." "No sweat Sir."[10]

Dave went on to say that if the major had been an Air Police officer, he might have received an Article 15 (commander's punishment) and lost a "stripe" for this incident. However, Dave's response was: "What was he going to do? Send me to Vietnam?"

Did you know the Air Force had a Navy? Dave Green said,

---

[9] Bertolet, "Letters Home from Vietnam," p. 38.
[10] Personal communication with Dave Green on March 8, 2004.

"Well, it wasn't exactly a navy; they were unarmed landing craft, the kind that dropped troops off on the beaches." The boats would meet ships bringing supplies into Vietnam and take them several miles up the river to an old French hanger ramp, where they would be off loaded. "Slick, huh? Of course it was Air Force and it needed A.P.s to guard the convoy." And that's how Dave ended up going up and down the Saigon River a few times.

The three main air bases in Vietnam in 1965 were Tan Son Nhut, Bien Hoa, and Da Nang. The 6250th APS was assigned to Tan Son Nhut, the 6251st APS was at Bien Hoa, and the 6252nd APS was located at Da Nang.[11] The Air Force would eventually have ten major bases in Vietnam. In addition, air/security police were detached, either TDY or PCS, to a number of radar sites such as the one at Dong Ha. During the Vietnam War, no air base guarded by Air Police/Security Police was ever overrun or captured by the enemy.

I had gone through M-16 training at Clark AB, Philippines on my way to Vietnam. I was qualified with the M-2 Carbine and 38 cal. pistol at my former base, but we had not yet been issued M-16s before I left for Vietnam. I remember going through the shotgun qualification course and night firing exercise at Tan Son Nhut. At the time, I did not know Sergeant Bradford or that he was the NCOIC of weapons training at Tan Son Nhut. TSgt. Sergeant Bradford and SSgt. Robert Riley provided training for all new Air Police, Ranch Hand crews[12], and other Air Force personnel with the M-16 rifle, M-60 machine gun, M-79 grenade launcher, hand grenades, and night firing exercises.

In the passages below, Sergeant Bradford describes how he got involved with weapons training:

> With the big military buildup in 1965, there was a need for a weapons training program. I was assigned to the Base Weapons Training Section in July. I was the Weapons NCO. There were not a lot of resources available and I soon realized that I would have to scrounge for weapons,

---

[11] Later redesignated the 377th APS, 3rd APS, and the 366th APS respectively. On May 1, 1967, all air police units were officially redesignated security police units.

[12] The Ranch Hand crews were the ones involved in aerial spraying of chemical defoliants (Agent Orange) in Vietnam.

ammunition, and a firing range. The first thing I did was to assemble a crew to get the job done. I asked for Robert Riley, a SSgt., whom I knew would do an outstanding job, which he did.

We got the word out to the First Sergeants of each unit to provide us with a training roster of personnel who would require the training. In addition to the new air policemen arriving at Tan Son Nhut, we trained the Ranch Hand crewmembers. These aircrews flew C-123s equipped for spray missions and were the ones responsible for the defoliation operation going on in Vietnam.

We found a place on base, an old French firing range, to set up our range. We got permission from the VNAF (Vietnamese Air Force) commander to use the range. However, we had to cut the elephant grass that had grown up through years of nonuse. I contacted a friend of mine in the Base Engineers who loaned me a young trooper to drive the tractor and bush hog. As he was clearing the field, a big—at least fifteen-foot—black Cobra came out of the bush. It scared the hell out of both of us and we got out of there real quick.

Nevertheless, the field was eventually cleared and the training commenced in earnest within a couple of days. We trained troops on the M-16 rifle and M-60 machine gun and other weapons, including both day and night firing. However, soon after our training started, the VNAF commander ordered the firing on the base to stop. I did some trading with the Army Special Forces troops at Bien Hoa and they let us set up our firing range near their camp. We also acquired several M-79s from the Special Forces and added

training in hand grenades. That is how we got things done in
Vietnam. If we had waited for requisitions to go through
official channels, we would never have gotten anything
accomplished.[13]

Sergeant Carl Bradford had been assigned to Tan Son Nhut in
early April 1965. David Green and Joseph Lee got to TSN in
May 1965. At that time, according to Dave Green, there were
only about forty or fifty air police in the entire squadron. Dave
Black was assigned to Tan Son Nhut also in May. Dave had had
a prior tour in Vietnam at Bien Hoa Air Base in 1964. John
Bertolet and Jim Schneider arrived at Tan Son Nhut at about the
same time as me, although we did not know one another at the
time. By July 1965, the squadron consisted of several hundred air
policemen and we were assigned to different flights (in the Air
Force a flight is equivalent to an Army platoon). Sam Baldon
arrived in Vietnam in late July or early August 1965. Ed Cheri got
to Tan Son Nhut in November, as did Jack Case and Bob
Stemock. Case and Stemock were initially assigned to the 4th Air
Commando Squadron. They had gone through two months of
commando training at Forbes AFB, Kansas, prior to coming to
Vietnam. After six weeks of escorting convoys and flying with
FAC (Forward Air Controllers) pilots in O1-E aircraft, they were
reassigned to the 6250th Air Police Squadron and subsequently
volunteered for the Dong Ha mission. As it turned out, it was our
gain, because the U.S. Army's 5th Special Forces had trained
Jack and Bob, and their training would be invaluable to the rest
of us. This group would go up to Dong Ha.

A copy of our orders[14] dated December 21, 1965 read in part:
"The following personnel are relieved from 6250 Air Police
Squadron this station; assigned 620 Tactical Control Squadron."

TSGT	Carl L. Bradford
A1C	Edward F. Cheri
A1C	Jack J. Case
A1C	Robert M. Stemock
A2C	David L. Black

[13] Bradford, "A Message to My Troops," p. 39.
[14] Special Order AB-111 dated December 21, 1965 from Headquarters 6250th Combat Support Group
(PACAF).

A2C	Samuel Baldon
A2C	John A. Bertolet
A2C	William D. Bland
A2C	David M. Green
A2C	Joseph L. Lee
A2C	James H. Schneider

Though no one remembers the exact date, we left Tan Son Nhut probably around the 27th or 28th of December. That would mean we were still at TSN on the 25th, however not one of the Bandits recall where or what they were doing on Christmas Day, 1965. It is as if that day disappeared from our lives.

I remember seeing the Bob Hope show before leaving Tan Son Nhut. Jim Schneider stated:

> One of my most memorable experiences at TSN was the Bob Hope Christmas Show for the troops in Vietnam. I had a great seat for the show, sitting just two or three rows behind General Westmoreland, Commanding General of U.S. Forces in Vietnam. The show included Miss America 1965, Anita Bryant, Kaye Stevens, and Carol Baker.[15]

Bob Hope, Tan Son Nhut, 1965

Several people mentioned seeing Miss America at the show, however I checked with the USO website archives and found that

---

[15] Personal communication with Jim Schneider on March 1, 2004.

Diana Lynn Batts was listed as Miss Virginia. Joey Heatherton was also one of the entertainers in the show. And of course, the 6250th APS provided security for the Bob Hope show while it was at Tan Son Nhut.

Bob Hope Show, Tan Son Nhut, 1965

A well-known landmark in downtown Saigon that was frequently visited by American servicemen was the My Cahn Floating Restaurant. The restaurant had a mystique of danger and the lure of excitement associated with it since it had been the target of an earlier terrorist attack.

My Cånh Restaurant, 1965

The My Canh Restaurant had been blown up in May of 1965, killing approximately forty American servicemen and Vietnamese civilians. The VC had placed a small explosive charge on the restaurant and a second, time-delayed, explosive device on the walkway from the restaurant to the dock. The second explosion killed the most people, as they were trying to leave the restaurant to go ashore.

Having visited Saigon on numerous occasions, I had developed a sense of what to do in a terrorist situation. The safest approach would have been not to go into Saigon, but that was not going to happen. The main thing was to be vigilant of your surroundings and to notice anything out of the ordinary. In addition to the hotel and bar bombings mentioned earlier in the chapter, a number of servicemen had been killed in taxicab explosions. As a rule, if the driver got out of the vehicle, you got out of the cab. I recall a specific incident in which that happened. We were stopped in heavy traffic and for no good reason the driver opened his door and got out. I got out too. I have no idea why he went to the back of the cab, but I didn't get back in until he did.

Hotel bombing in Saigon, 1965

Though Saigon was not the safest place to be, we were on our way to an outpost just ten miles from the DMZ. John Bertolet recalled:

In a small group meeting before we left Tan San Nhut, Sarge told us to cash in our BX cards for all the liquor that we could get. He went on to say that we were going to need some supplies that the Air Force did not have. The idea was to trade the liquor for grenades and other things to the Marines at Da Nang on our way up to Dong Ha. We did what he asked without question.[16]

We flew up to Da Nang and spent a couple of nights on the air base in an area known as Camp Da Nang before heading up to Dong Ha. When we arrived at Da Nang, the APs from the 6252nd Air Police Squadron had no idea who we were. Some of us were dressed in camouflaged fatigues and jungle boots and wearing our Blue Berets with the QC patch. At the time, the 6250th APS was the only Air Force unit wearing the beret. Dave Green remembered being "chewed out" by the 6252nd Commander for being out of uniform.

The town of Da Nang was off limits, but somehow I managed to get off the base. I am not sure who was with me, but we had a rather bizarre encounter with a Vietnamese man. He came running down an alley behind us screaming something in Vietnamese. I didn't understand what he was saying, but felt threatened that he was after us; I pulled out my bayonet and turned to face him. He immediately stopped in his tracks and retreated in the other direction. I am not sure if it was the bayonet or if he saw the QC patch that persuaded him to make a hasty retreat.

The time we spent in Da Nang brought us closer together as a group and we were about to get our nickname "Bandits." When we left Tan Son Nhut we were armed only with our M-16s and one 20-round magazine each. By the time we left Da Nang, we had at least ten or more magazines and several grenades each. Bandits we were and the name stuck.

---

[16] Bertolet, "Letters Home from Vietnam," p. 42.

Arrival at Dong Ha

Dong Ha Air Base was constructed in late November and the radar site was activated on November 25, 1965. It was an air base in name only. While there was a short, dirt, airstrip, no planes other than a "Bird-dog" spotter aircraft (O1-E) were assigned to Dong Ha. It was a remote, forward radar site designated Det. 1, 620th Tactical Control Squadron. The 620th TCS was located at Monkey Mountain near Da Nang Air Base and was part of a series of radar sites operating under the 505th Tactical Control Group at Tan Son Nhut Air Base. The call sign for Dong Ha was "Waterboy." It was the northernmost American base in 1965.

Bradford's Bandits, a small group of U.S. Air Force combat police, were assigned to Dong Ha in December 1965 to secure the site. We were the "grunts" of the Air Force and proud of it. We wore Air Force chevrons, but we were the ones who secured the perimeter of this small, remote outpost near the DMZ separating North and South Vietnam. At that time, the nearest American combat force was located forty miles south at Phu Bai. Thus, we were pretty much on our own to defend the air base. Later in the war, Dong Ha would become a large Marine combat base, but we were there first.

We were the first unit of air police to be permanently assigned (PCS) to Dong Ha. We replaced a small group of air police that had been temporarily assigned (TDY) to Dong Ha. They had been at Dong Ha for about a month when we got there. They left Dong Ha on the same plane that brought us in. We had very little time with this group since the plane took off almost immediately. That brief encounter on the runway was all the contact we had with them.

John Bertolet had the following to say about that first day at Dong Ha:

> When we landed at Dong Ha, the security forces that were
> there pulled up stakes and left on the same plane that brought
> us in. We were left with no knowledge of the lay of the land,
> no information about guard posts, weapons that had been left
> for us, or what to watch out for. They just got out! We were
> on our own. From that moment on, Sergeant Bradford took
> command. That first night we picked up our M16s, our
> grenades, our magazines filled with bullets, and paired up
> and walked out to a bunker and went to work.[1]

I believe we flew into Dong Ha on a C-123 on December 31,
1965. One of my clearest memories of Dong Ha was going out on
post on New Year's Eve, 1965. That date is corroborated by photos
taken by Sam Baldon of Da Nang Harbor from the airplane.

The morning after we came off our first night of guard duty, we
were called into Sergeant Bradford's tent. Sarge had a bottle of
Jim Beam; he took a swallow, then passed it around to all the
Bandits. We did not have any glasses, so everyone drank from the
bottle. We sat on the floor and passed the bottle around until it
was completely consumed, and one by one the Bandits fell
asleep.

Jim Schneider, Dave Green, and John Bertolet

---

[1] Bertolet, John A. "Letters Home from Vietnam," *Tiger Flight, 13* (4), 2004, pp. 37-42.

The radar unit had received several 50-cal. machine guns; however, when we arrived at Dong Ha, they were still in crates. TSgt. Bradford assigned A1C Case and A1C Stemock the task of making the 50s operational. The 50-cals. were placed on the southeast and southwest corners of the site and a third was located on the northeast corner. Eventually, a 50-cal. was placed on the northwest corner as well. We also had a Light Anti-Tank Weapon (LAW). Other weapons included M-60s, an M-79 grenade launcher, M-16s, at least one shotgun, and several .45 and .38 cal. pistols. The M-60 bunkers were placed between the 50-cal. positions; however, when we first got to Dong Ha, we did not man the north wall. It was protected by ARVN (Army of the Republic of Vietnam) troops, but after the first mortar attack we reinforced all four sides. The only entrance into the compound was a gate on the west side. There was a minefield along the east and south berms, along with claymore mines that we controlled from our bunkers. The perimeter was fenced with several rows of barbed wire. There was a 35-foot clearing between the bunkers and the minefield. The berm was a ten-foot high wall of dirt embedded with sandbag bunkers. In addition to our posts, airmen from the radar unit were armed with M-16 rifles and filled in along the berm when the base came under attack.

Claymore mines were positioned facing outward toward the perimeter. Sandbags were place behind the mine to prevent Charlie from turning it around so it would explode back at us. Each air police bunker controlled several claymore mines.

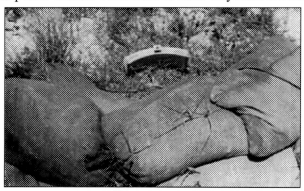

Claymore mine

In 1965, I believe we were the first air police unit in Vietnam to be armed with the 50-cal. machine gun and the first to actually fire the gun in combat (January 8, 1966).[2] Fortunately for us, TSgt. Bradford had been in charge of weapons training at TSN prior to our being assigned to Dong Ha. He trained us on the 50-cal. machine gun, M-60, M-79, hand grenades, and other weapons. Each man could operate any weapon or take over any job in the unit. In addition, A1C Case and A1C Stemock had received two months of Air Commando training at Forbes AFB, Kansas immediately prior to coming to Vietnam. They taught the rest of us about overlapping fields of fire, how to operate the claymore mines, and small-unit tactics.

View of the east perimeter

In reference to his commando training provided by the Army's 5th Special Forces, Bob Stemock remarked, "We were trained in military tactics; how to react if ambushed in a convoy, weapons, explosives, and unarmed combat. Just enough to probably get us killed!"[3] Nevertheless, that training came in handy at Dong Ha. Bob described our first night on post. "We were all on our posts within hours of landing. I guess we were all pretty scared that

[2] Bland, William D. "Bradford's Bandits: A Tribute to Carl Bradford, MSgt. (Ret.) and His Defenders of Dong Ha Air Base, Vietnam, 1965-1966." *Tiger Flight, 11* (16), 2002, pp. 37-41.
[3] Personal communication with Bob Stemock on March 12, 2004.

first night since we had no idea what to expect."[4]

My very first memory of Dong Ha was digging the trench around the mound where the 50 cal. would be placed. As I looked around the countryside, I thought: This was not Tan Son Nhut. We were all alone up here and Charlie (Viet Cong) was all around us.

Jack Case and Ed Cheri teamed up and manned one of the 50 cal. machine gun posts on the southeast corner of the compound.

Back view of 50 cal. bunker on the southeast corner

There was another 50 cal. post located on the northeast corner. This post covered the east side of the compound including the area between the camp and Highway 1. A third 50 cal. position covered the south perimeter looking out toward the dirt runway.

Though Dong Ha was an air base in name only, there was one O1-E aircraft flown by an Air Force Forward Air Controller. The FAC mission was to spot enemy forces on the ground and to guide fighter-bombers to their location. At Dong Ha, the plane was rolled up to the Air Force compound; it did not stay on the runway, which was unguarded at night.

---

[4] *Ibid,* Bob Stemock.

Joe Lee and John Bertolet

TSgt. Bradford was our NCOIC and "Top Cop" at Dong Ha. Yet, none of us remember him ever barking out orders. He led by example and if he asked us to do something, we did it. There was very little distinction among the troops based on rank. We worked together as a team, each counting on the other to perform his job. That teamwork paid off when the first attack occurred on Dong Ha, and continued throughout our tour. No one took credit for individual accomplishments. We did things as a team, with each person contributing to the mission. We may have been called "Bandits," but we did not have any slackers in our outfit.

As Air Police, our primary mission at Dong Ha was to provide ground defense for the air base. We were dug in along the perimeter. The most stressful part of guarding the perimeter was looking for VC (Viet Cong) moving through the wire. We also had the threat of an all-out attack. We were on post from just before sunset until after sunrise every night. We manned the bunkers at night; however we were on duty 24/7. We also took turns manning the main gate during the day. It was only in the latter part of our tour when reinforcements arrived at Dong Ha that we ever got a night off. We averaged only about four hours of sleep a day. During the rest of the day, we built and rebuilt sandbag bunkers, began the construction of the underground command post, cleaned our weapons, and got ready for going back out on post. We also performed other security duties such as escorting convoys to Quang Tri. In the evening, just before taking our posts, we rotated going out on three-man jeep patrols (with mounted M-60) around the outside perimeter of the air base.

Bill Bland cleaning his weapon

Supply planes flew in during the day, but left immediately after dropping off their cargo. We did not guard the airfield at night. It was left to Charlie (VC) to do with as he pleased. Nevertheless, ARVN troops drove up and down the dirt airstrip in the morning searching for mines or other explosives. The vehicle floorboard was reinforced with sandbags; however we often wondered how these Vietnamese soldiers were assigned to that duty.

Dave Green, 50 cal. located on northeast corner facing Highway 1

On one occasion, we went to the aid of a U.S. Marine helicopter that had been forced to land at Dong Ha at night. The helicopter had been hit by enemy gunfire. We secured the airfield prior to its arrival and then escorted the Marines to the main compound.

In Vietnam and other wars, U.S. Marines have rescued numerous Air Force pilots from enemy forces. However, this was probably the first and maybe the only time that Air Force ground troops secured a landing for a Marine aircraft in a combat zone. I remember the Marine pilot saying that he had been in Vietnam for five days and that this was his first combat mission.

By the end of 1965, U.S. armed forces in Vietnam numbered approximately 150,000; however, the North Vietnamese had also increased the number of personnel and equipment entering the war in the South—mainly along the Ho Chi Minh Trail on the border between Vietnam and Laos. Enemy forces operating in the South now numbered approximately 250,000, including 36,000 NVA regulars. The South Vietnamese forces numbered approximately 300,000 troops.

After several major defeats by American forces, enemy tactics were also changing. Instead of confronting large American combat units directly, the North Vietnamese launched guerrilla assaults and ambushes on smaller units and used hit-and-run attacks on more isolated and usually less well-defended outposts.

At Dong Ha, the U.S. Air Force had about 150 troops and the South Vietnamese Army unit was composed of approximately two hundred soldiers from the 1st ARVN Division. There was at least one NVA division (10,000 soldiers) and approximately five hundred to fifteen hundred VC located within the surrounding area.

The buildup of American forces in Vietnam had occurred from the middle of July until the end of 1965. There was one advantage that we had and that was that most of our senior NCOs had served in the Korean War and some had been in WWII. Their experience and confidence boosted morale among the younger airmen. And of course, the Bandits had Sergeant Bradford as our leader. Though he was too young to have served in Korea, he had joined the Alabama Army National Guard and had received infantry training. His specialized training in weapons would come in handy at Dong Ha.

On Christmas Day in 1965, the United States had stopped the bombing over North Vietnam in an effort to appease the North Vietnamese into peace negotiations. The ceasefire did not last very long. Our first combat experience would occur on January 8, 1966, nine days after we had arrived at Dong Ha. Bombing would resume on January 31, 1966.[5]

---

[5] Air Force Historical Research Agency, Maxwell AFB, AL. "Vietnam Service 1958-1973." Retrieved March 15, 2004 from http://www.au.af.mil/afhra.

Our First Mortar Attack

We had been at Dong Ha less than two weeks before our first mortar attack. Based on a letter written home by John Bertolet, the first attack occurred on January 8, 1966.[1] All of the air police were on post when the mortar rounds began hitting Dong Ha. There was also some small arms fire coming from the area near the airstrip. Both 50-cal. positions along the south berm opened fire, spraying the valley between the airfield and us. The 50-cals. provided suppressing fire support for ARVN troops that were guarding a TAC antenna site located near the airstrip. Case and Cheri were on the 50-cal. located on the southeast corner of the berm and Black and Baldon were on the other 50-cal. located on the southwest corner. Dave Black observed a small number of VC outside the wire between the airstrip and the southwest area of the compound. He and Sam Baldon fired on the VC with their 50-cal., halting the enemy's advance. Bertolet and myself manned a bunker between the two 50s on the south berm. We could hear the rounds going over our heads and hitting behind us and we saw the fireballs (forever etched in my memory) of at least five or six rounds hit right in front of our bunker. When the mortar rounds stopped, we fixed bayonets and waited for a ground assault.

It was our first combat experience and I am sure everyone was a little afraid, but nobody panicked. I recall thinking back to all the war movies I had seen when I was growing up. One movie stood out. I don't remember the name, but it was about a small unit of Marines in Korea that was pinned down by thousands of Chinese troops. The Marines were spread out thin along a ridge, and all during the night Chinese soldiers were trying to penetrate the perimeter. Years later, in Vietnam, I felt as if I was in the movie rather than watching it.

[1] Bertolet, John A. "Letters Home from Vietnam," *Tiger Flight, 13* (4), 2004, pp. 37-42.

The day before the attack, Bertolet and I had torn down our bunker and were in the process of rebuilding it; we had only three or four rows of sandbags that formed the walls, but no top to the bunker. When the mortar rounds began hitting Dong Ha, we ran to the nearest bunker to seek shelter from the barrage. The next day we worked hard to finish the bunker before going back on post that night.

View of the south berm

For the remainder of the night however, we stayed on alert. In addition, airmen from the radar unit manned bunkers along the berm. All of the airmen at Dong Ha were armed with M-16 rifles and served as riflemen in defense of the base; however, air police had primary responsibility for security and defense of the base. Air police manned the machine gun bunkers and key defensive positions. We were on the berm at night while the radar airmen slept or were on duty manning the radar site.

The rest of the night was rather long and tense, waiting to see if an all-out attack would follow. An AC-47 from Da Nang showed up and dropped flares to light up the area. I remember thinking earlier in the evening, how nice the night was. After standing guard during many dark and rainy nights, I was pleased to see the moonlight. Since it made our job of watching the perimeter easier, I did not think about the fact that the VC mortar crews could see us as well.[2]

[2] Bland, William D. "The Little Alamo: Dong Ha Air Base, Vietnam, 1956-1966." *Tiger Flight*, *8* (4), 1999, pp. 31-32.

Imagine thirty to thirty-five rounds of 81mm mortar landing in an area only about 250 yards long and 150 yards wide, to give you some idea of the impact of the rounds. Mortars were landing all around us. Fortunately, we had no causalities; however, almost every structure on the site had some damage. One mortar round went through the top of a tent and through the wood floor without detonating. From the outside, our tent looked okay, but inside, the sunlight revealed numerous holes from just above the cots to the ceiling. However, since we (APs) were always on the berm at night, no one was in the tent during the attack. One ARVN soldier was killed and three were wounded during the attack.

The next morning, Case, Cheri, Stemock, and Black recovered and destroyed several mortar rounds that had failed to explode on impact. This was beyond the call of duty for air policemen; normally, ordinance disposal experts would have performed this kind of dangerous work. They were each awarded the Air Force Commendation Medal.

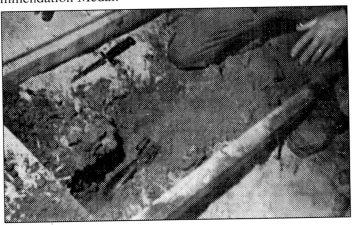

Unexploded mortar round

Bob Stemock talked about his experience:

Jack Case, Ed Cheri, Dave Black and myself spent the morning clearing the compound of unexploded mortar rounds. Jack and I had received explosives training at Forbes

AFB but not EOD training. However, it had to be done and there was no one else immediately available. I guess that's the way Jack and I ended up in charge of the minefields. I can still remember mixing a chemical, which I later found out was a barrel of Agent Orange, with diesel fuel to spray on the no man's land between the berm and the outer fence line in order to kill the vegetation. The grass and bushes would grow and pull the trip wire pins on the mines. Neither Jack nor I appreciated having to go and replace them.[3]

There is some dispute concerning the number of incoming mortar rounds. To my knowledge, there are no official Air Force documents for Det. 1, 620th TCS at Dong Ha. Those records either were not kept or have been lost over the years. In my description above, I approximated the number of rounds to be between thirty and thirty-five based on the "Little Alamo" story that had reported a combined sixty-five rounds in the two attacks on January 8, 1966 and February 4, 1966. In a letter John Bertolet wrote home on January 14, 1966, he told his parents, "You asked how safe I am up here. I can tell you this; I will never forget the night of January 8, 1966. We received seventeen rounds of 81mm mortar fire."[4] John is not certain how he came up with that number (seventeen rounds). I am not sure either; however, I know I saw at least five or six rounds hit directly in front of the bunker I shared with John. I was aware that rounds were going over our heads and hitting behind us, but at the moment I was focused on the perimeter, in anticipation of a ground attack once the mortars stopped.

Jim Schneider gave this personal account of that first mortar attack:

On January 8, 1966, Dong Ha received numerous rounds of 60mm and 81mm mortars. I remember being on duty that night and standing outside my post on the berm. I believe that I was on the 50 cal. machine gun bunker located on the

---

[3] Personal communication with Bob Stemock on March 12, 2004.
[4] Bertolet, "Letters Home from Vietnam," p. 39.

northeast corner of the Air Force compound. I was looking out over the perimeter when all of a sudden there was a flash of light coming from the ARVN (South Vietnamese Army) compound directly behind us. At first I didn't know what was happening. However, when the second mortar round came in, I realized the Viet Cong (VC) or North Vietnamese Army (NVA) was attacking us. I jumped inside the bunker for protection. I felt a little safer inside the bunker, but I still didn't know what was going to follow the mortar attack. I was behind the 50 cal. machine gun, waiting for a possible ground assault. I don't remember if anyone was with me on that night or not. I believe Dave Green and Joe Lee were in a bunker position between my post and the 50 cal. located on the southeast corner.[5]

It would have been unusual for Jim to be posted on a machine gun bunker by himself; however, Jim does not remember who was with him on that post during the attack. We have tried to account for where each person was located that night. Neither Joe Lee nor Dave Green remember exactly where they were, thus we assumed that they were on post together (because most of the time, they worked together). I believe they were on the east berm, halfway between the two 50 cal. positions on the northeast and southeast corners.

Bob Stemock recalled:

The first mortar attack came on a Saturday night, the 8th of January. I remember it clearly because I was going to work the Main Gate the next morning and was in bed when a loud explosion erupted. I jumped up, wondering if it was the 105 Howitzers going off in the ARVN compound next to ours. The next thing I knew, there was a flash, like a camera flashbulb except much brighter, and then a large fireball appeared approximately thirty to forty yards from our tent. I knew what that was and I grabbed my clothes, M-16, and

---

[5] Personal communication with Jim Schneider on March 11, 2004.

gear and ran to the bunker located immediately behind our tent. I dressed and spent the remainder of the night in the bunker looking out over the minefield. I believe there was a Spooky (AC-47 Gunship) in the area and it dropped flares throughout the night.[6]

The nearest Air Police bunker behind our tent that Bob would most likely have gone to, would have been the 50 cal. position manned by Jim Schneider on the northeast corner. Bob was the only AP that was not on the berm when the rounds started coming in. I had always thought Bob was in the command post. However, the first attack occurred before our underground CP was built.

After this attack, the filling and toting of sandbags became a familiar site around Dong Ha as we reinforced our bunker positions along the perimeter.

Rifle bunker on the south berm

I am not positive, and neither is Sergeant Bradford, but I believe that he was at Tan Son Nhut during the first attack. As I recall, Sarge returned the next day with a number of M-60 machine guns. I know that on the night of the first attack, John Bertolet and I were armed only with M-16 rifles. In addition, the next morning, we were in the process of rebuilding our bunker

[6] Personal communication with Bob Stemock on March 12, 2004.

when a Lieutenant (it might have been Lt. Richard) ordered us to go to the north wall to build bunkers. I attempted to explain to the Lt. that we needed to complete our bunker before we went back out on post that evening. He became quite upset and yelled that we would obey his order. At that point, I distinctly remember telling Bert to get Sergeant Bradford; thus he had to have been at Dong Ha when this incident occurred. I also know that we did not go to the north wall. The only explanation is that Sergeant Bradford intervened on our behalf because he was the only one that could have stood up to the Lieutenant.

One week after the first mortar attack, three rounds hit near the southeast part of the airstrip, but no rounds landed inside the compound. The next morning, we were fortifying our positions along the berm when I was called to the tent of Major Cummings (the site commander). I reported to him in a military fashion, but the Major responded more like a father than a commander. He informed me that my brother had been killed in a car accident and that my family had requested, via the Red Cross, that I be given emergency leave. Major Cummings told me that I would be on the first flight out of Dong Ha. I do not remember much after that, except that I was home within a couple of days. The following is an excerpt from a letter dated January 27, 1966 that I wrote to the Bandits while I was at home on leave: "It's sort of strange, but I have been more scared since I have been home, looking back, than I was in Vietnam. But things are beginning to bore me, and I eagerly await my return to the war."

Also, while I was home, I received a letter from John Bertolet telling me about the big mortar attack on February 4, 1966. I got back to Dong Ha on February 23, 1966. All my stuff was exactly where I had left it when I left Dong Ha. Even though I was not physically with them, I was there in spirit. While I was home, the Bandits were always in my heart and in my thoughts. I was glad to be back with the guys. I was also sorry that I was not there with them during the VC mortar attack in February. I had good reason to be away, but I always felt a little guilty for being safe while they were in danger.

The Little Alamo

After the second big attack on Dong Ha, the radar site was being referred to as the "Little Alamo" and received quite a bit of press coverage, including an article in *The Air Division Advisor* (2nd Air Division).[1] The following is an account of the February attack on Dong Ha by John Bertolet:

On the evening of the 4th of February at about 11:00 p.m., I was standing outside of my sandbag bunker looking down into the valley. Then came the sound I had heard three times before. It was the sound of mortar shells being dropped into the tube and streaking into flight. I heard about six or eight booms within less than fifteen seconds. I knew just what to do. I ran into my bunker, alerted my friend inside and put on my helmet. By that time, the first shells were landing. I pulled my M-60 machine gun inside to protect it. In the same amount of time it took to send them, all of the 81mm mortar shells landed. They missed their mark—they fell short and too far east. There was a pause for about thirty seconds. Then the VC opened up from a different direction putting twelve rounds in the 155mm cannon area of the Vietnamese compound directly behind us. By that time, the first tubes had re-aimed and about five rounds landed into the compound. After a short pause from the first tube, the VC opened up again. This time, the rounds fell about twenty yards short of the berm but they were walking them down to me. The last round landed about seventy-five feet in front of my bunker. I heard the pieces of mortar pass over the bunker.

[1] Horne, TSgt. Charles E. "Airmen Defend Little Radar Site: They Call It Little Alamo." *The Air Division Advisor, 2* (8), March 4, 1966, pp.1, 4.

Needless to say my head was down real low. Even before the VC shelling had stopped, the 155s Howitzers were barking back at them. I could hear the 155 rounds pass over my head and land about two and a half or three miles out. I hoped that they were on target. The 155s popped out about thirty rounds, and the 81s lobbed about sixty-five rounds back at the VC. In the Vietnamese compound located directly behind us, they had both 81mm mortars and 155mm Howitzers, which they fired back at the VC.

John continued:

Sounds like fun doesn't it. Well it wasn't. The first round that landed in our compound cut my telephone line. It landed in the middle of a road, causing no other damage. The second round landed in a ditch behind the mess hall within five feet of the spot a mortar landed during the last attack. That one did no damage. The third round landed on top of a fourteen hundred dollar freezer unit placed next to the mess hall. A number of mortar pieces hit the wall of the mess hall. The fourth round landed at the door in front of the mess hall. That round was a dud. The site commander was lucky; he had moved from that location just the week before the attack. The last round to land in the compound came through the top of a tent; it split the center pole, glanced off a locker and went through a 5/8 inch piece of plywood flooring and then eight inches of earth.[2]

---

[2] Bertolet, John A. "Letters Home from Vietnam." *Tiger Flight, 13* (4) 2004, pp. 37-42.

34

ARVN 105mm Howitzer

In the above passage, John refers to the ARVN artillery as a 155mm Howitzer. Jim Schneider also described it as a 155mm. However, I always thought it was a 105mm Howitzer. Bob Stemock said it was a 105mm, not a 155mm Howitzer. We were military police, not artillerymen. John took a photo of the ARVN troops who were located in the compound directly behind us; however, this photo was not necessarily taken right after the February attack. It is possible that on some occasions, the ARVN did have a 155mm Howitzer.

Most of us (A2Cs) had enlisted in the Air Force right after high school, and had been in the service for two years before volunteering for Vietnam. Thus, when we got to Dong Ha, we were either twenty or twenty-one at the time. The February attack occurred just a couple of days before Jim Schneider's twenty-first birthday. Below is what Jim had to say about the mortar attack:

> On February 4, 1966, VC or NVA mortar crews attacked us
> again. This attack also occurred at night while we were on
> duty. Since the first mortar attack, I tended to stay inside the
> bunker rather than outside of it. This attack was a little more
> personal for me as it occurred only two days before my

twenty-first birthday. I planned on being around to celebrate, thus I stayed in the bunker. Numerous rounds landed in the ARVN compound behind me. The ARVN soldiers fired 155mm Howitzer artillery rounds back at the North Vietnamese. I don't believe we had any casualties but I remember that a mortar round landed inside a tent, went through the wood floor, and did not explode.[3]

Col. Daniel and Lt. Col. Meyer inspecting 50 cal. machine gun post

After the attack, Colonel Charles L. Daniel (505th Tactical Control Group Commander) and Lt. Colonel William S. Meyer (620th Tactical Control Squadron Commander) visited the Dong Ha site. They inspected Dong Ha defenses, including the 50 cal. machine gun bunker on the southeast corner. Lt. D. L. Richard ("Cowboy"), the security officer for Dong Ha was also present. The post was manned by Ed Cheri and another AP named Mike Post. Mike was one of the replacements that came up in February or March 1966.

---

[3] Personal communication with Jim Schneider on March 11, 2004.

On March 6, 1966, John Bertolet, in a letter home to his parents, sent a Teletype report that told the story about the "Little Alamo." The report read as follows:

> Little Alamo Radar Site[4]
> Only 10 Miles from Red Border
> Dong Ha, Vietnam (OI) - - They call the place "Little Alamo." It's a U. S. Air Force radar site, its northernmost outpost 10 miles south of the border with communist North Vietnam.
>
> Officially the name of the site is Dong Ha, and "they" are the officers and airmen who man and protect the tiny site. The history of "Little Alamo" closely resembles the plight experienced by the true Alamo but with one difference.
>
> That difference is the two attacks that both Alamos underwent. The famous Alamo was attacked in February 1836, and overrun March 6.
>
> The "Little Alamo" beat off two Viet Cong mortar attacks in January and February 1966. Even though the communists lobbed in 65 rounds of 81mm mortar shells, not a single airman was hit.
>
> Within its boundary are complicated and intricate radar antenna consoles, scopes and the headquarters of the Det. 1, 620th Tactical Control Group. Commander of Det. 1 is Maj. Lawrence Cummings of Baytown, Tex. Personnel here have two primary missions. They guide the hundreds of aircraft flying missions in their area. They defend the site. Each officer and airman at Dong Ha has completed Base Defense Combat Training, and the Air Police who are the

---

[4] Horne. "Airmen Defend Little Radar Site," pp. 1, 4.

first line of defense took Combat Commando Training at Forbes, AFB, Kan.

The airmen have built a defense perimeter that is one of the most sophisticated to be found in Vietnam. It consists of several types of mines, rolled barbed wire, a 35-foot clearing and a high dirt wall that is imbedded with different types of defensive and offensive weapons.

During the last mortar siege, two communist 81mm mortar shells destroyed the two cold storage reefers there and 1,045 pounds of meat.

In spite of the hardships airmen endure here daily, morale is exceptionally high. An important element is teamwork. Each airman speaks well of cooperative efforts with his buddies. For example, someone with electrical experience helped to wire all tents for electricity, which is produced by mobile generators. Radar technicians volunteer to help the defense guards with their 12-hour shifts of sentry duty.

With all the drawbacks of field living conditions and the strain of long hours of labor, airmen here find time to be humorous. An example is the sign placed in front of the tents. It reads, "Mortar Square, Vacancy in Shrapnel Apartments."

When the men are not at their duty stations, they spend time repairing damaged areas, building additional underground defenses and cleaning equipment...

Mortar damage to the mess hall

War is a horrific experience; however, not every moment is spent in combat. Just a few days after the February battle, a picture was taken of Dave Black and Jack Case giving some chewing gum to a little Vietnamese girl from the village of Dong Ha.

Dave Black and Jack Case

A couple of weeks after the attack, John Bertolet was interviewed by another reporter. John said:

> An Air Force combat reporter interviewed me on February 17th. His name was James Conley. He taped the interview and said that it would be aired over a radio station in my area back home in a few weeks. When I got home, my folks told me that the Charleston radio station called them to let them know when it would play. They said that it was good to hear my voice.[5]

The VC had hit Dong Ha hard, but the base was protected, thanks to the Bandits. We manned the machine gun bunkers and directed fire back at Charlie. Though this book is primarily about the Bandits, we were not alone in defending the base. The airmen from the radar squadron took up positions as riflemen right alongside us. Together, we defended the "Little Alamo." TSgt. Charles Horne wrote in *The Air Division Advisor:* "The Navy, Marines, and Army now have aircraft, at Dong Ha, the Air Force has its 'Infantry.'"[6]

On the 19th day of May 1966, the Governor of Texas, John Connally, declared[7] that all airmen at the Air Force installation at "Little Alamo," Vietnam were "commissioned honorary Texas citizens, en masse, with all rights, privileges, and emoluments appertaining to..."

---

[5] Bertolet, "Letters Home from Vietnam," p. 40.

[6] Horne, "Airmen Defend Little Radar Site," p. 4.

[7] Seal of State affixed at the city of Austin on May 19, 1966.

Life at Dong Ha

After that big February attack, things quieted down somewhat, or maybe we had just become more accustomed to the rigors of war. We would have an occasional mortar attack consisting of only two or three rounds; however, sporadic small arms fire and sniper fire would continue to harass Dong Ha. Then, in late May 1966, the NVA 324B Division (10,000 troops) was located in the DMZ poised to begin a major offensive in Quang Tri Province. We went on post every night in anticipation of and prepared for an all-out attack. There was no place to retreat; thus we would have defended the base to the last man. However, we had no doubt that if such an attack occurred, we would all have been killed.

Dong Ha in early 1966 was an Air Force forward radar site. It was a remote outpost with a dirt airstrip, defended by approximately 120 to 150 airmen.[1] Though it would later become a large Marine combat base, the Air Force had been there since November 1965. It was the northernmost U.S. military base at the time, approximately ten miles from the DMZ. The defense of Dong Ha rested solely on us and the other airmen from the radar squadron. Khe Sahn, at that time, was only an Army Special Forces camp and the nearest Marine base was located forty miles south at Phu Bai. The buildup of Marines at Dong Ha and at other camps located near the DMZ did not begin until Operation Hastings started in mid-July 1966. However, in March, a Marine platoon from the 3rd Battalion, 4th Marines at Phu Bai arrived at Dong Ha to help us secure the site. We welcomed the Marines and got along quite well with them. After all, APs were the grunts of the Air Force. We manned the perimeter together and also went outside the wire at night with the Marines on ambush details. The Marines were at Dong Ha for only a couple of weeks and then left almost as suddenly as they had arrived. Once

[1] Bland, William D. "The Little Alamo: Dong Ha Air Base, Vietnam, 1965-1966." *Tiger Flight, 8* (4), 1999, pp. 31-32.

again, we had sole responsibility for defending the base.

At night we could watch the recon planes taking pictures over the Ho Chi Minh Trail. Usually, within a matter of minutes, tracer rounds from anti-aircraft guns were observed. Khe Sahn, which was an Army Special Forces camp at the time, would receive almost nightly mortar fire. We could hear the bombs going off and small arms fire in the distance. There was not an evening when you didn't hear machine gun fire happening somewhere around Dong Ha. The war was so close, yet so far away; however, we never knew when we would be the target. The Viet Cong hit us often enough that we had to keep up a constant vigil against an enemy attack.

As air police assigned to the radar unit, we came under the command of the Det. 1, 620th TCS; nevertheless, while Sergeant Bradford was at Dong Ha, acting upon authority of Colonel Black, Chief of Air Police, 2nd Air Division, he was completely in charge of security operations. Sergeant Bradford also had a good working relationship with Major Cummings, the radar site commander.

Dong Ha was a remote outpost in 1965 and early 1966, but we did have a few celebrities make their way up to our camp. Three separate USO tours, including several football players, actors, singers, and comedians entertained the troops at Dong Ha. This was while I was home on leave, however Jim Schneider recalled:

> In either January or early February, Robert Mitchum, Johnny Unitas, and Roosevelt Grier were at Dong Ha. Also, I remember seeing Dean Jones and Ann Margaret, but I am not sure when it was.[2] These USO tours were well received by all the airmen at Dong Ha. There was not a lot to do at Dong Ha except work and sleep.[3]

Others cited that Frank Gifford and Willie Davis were with Unitas on his trip to Dong Ha.

The famous movie actor Robert Mitchum also came up to Dong Ha to visit with the troops. Accordingly, he received VIP

---

[2] Ann Margaret entertained the troops at Da Nang Air Base, March 13, 1966.
[3] Personal communication with Jim Schneider on March 11, 2004.

treatment everywhere he went. A couple of the guys also mentioned that the ex-football player Roosevelt Grier accompanied Mr. Mitchum on this trip.

Sam Baldon providing personal security for Mr. Mitchum

Despite the fact that we had responsibility for guarding the perimeter at night, air police gladly provided security for these special events during the day. Air police armed with an M-79 grenade launcher, M-16 rifles, and M-60 machine guns escorted Mr. Mitchum to Quang Tri City. It was alleged that Mitchum did not want to put on a flack jacket on his journey back to Quang Tri. Nonetheless, someone persuaded him to wear one for his protection before the convoy took off.

Dave Green and unidentified Air Policeman

We had a number of other celebrities come up to Dong Ha, including actor Dean Jones, singer Shannon Hale, and comedian Mickey O'Shanessy. They entertained the troops in the outdoor theatre. While these visits were very much appreciated, they were short-lived.

There was nothing better at Dong Ha than mail call. Letters from home were read and re-read and often shared with others. It took about ten days for mail sent from the states to reach us. John Bertolet recalled:

> My mom had sent me a box of cookies and I shared them with the other guys. Everyone said they were good. Even though I was ten thousand miles away, my mom's cookies gave me a sense of home.[4]

Letters and packages from home were the only contact we had with the outside world. We did not have television or have access to a radio station like the "Good Morning Vietnam" program broadcasted by the Armed Forces network in Saigon. Instead, we listened to "Hanoi Hannah." We enjoyed the music and did not pay much attention to the propaganda, though we often laughed at some of her outlandish commentary. On several occasions, Hanoi Hannah mentioned us (the radar site at Dong Ha) by name.

I tried to write home as often as I could, but if I didn't have the time to write, I just wrote "okay" or simply "ok" on a post card and sent it out with the mail plane. When I got home from Vietnam, my mother told me that the postman would say, "he's okay," when he delivered the mail. In those days, the mail was delivered to the front door and I am sure my mother was waiting anxiously each day to hear that I was okay. I am sure all mothers felt that way about their sons. In my particular case, my oldest brother was killed while I was in Vietnam and I know that my mother worried about losing another son.

Bertolet expressed similar sentiments:

> While I was in Vietnam, I wrote home to my folks but not as often as I should have or they wished. My parents were very

[4] Bertolet, John A. "Letters Home from Vietnam." *Tiger Flight, 13,* (4), 2004, pp. 37-41.

worried about me. They wanted me to write often to reassure them that I was safe. Postage was not a problem because all we had to do was to write "Free" on the envelope. For American servicemen, all mail postmarked from Vietnam was delivered free by the post office.[5]

In fact, you didn't even have to have a post card. You could tear the back off a C-ration box and use it to write a note home.

I felt, like all the Bandits did, that it was my duty to be in Vietnam, but I also wanted to go home. I can only imagine now what it was like for Sarge and Doc who had families of their own. Sarge's youngest child, his daughter Kelly, was only two years old at the time. When you are single and twenty years old, that is just something you don't think about. In the 1960s, it was extremely rare for airmen in their first enlistment to be married.

As I mentioned above, the base had an outdoor theatre where the airmen from the radar unit were able to see a movie at night— something that we rarely had the opportunity to do because we were usually on the perimeter at night.

A typical workday was about sixteen hours. Nevertheless, we got an occasional opportunity to go into the village of Dong Ha. Jim Schneider commented on the working conditions at Dong Ha and how he found some time to enjoy the local food:

> We worked fifteen to sixteen or more hours a day. When we were not on guard duty at night, we were fortifying our positions with sandbags. The rest of the time was spent sleeping, although on a few occasions I went into the village of Dong Ha during the day. I remember having lunch one day at a Vietnamese restaurant. I was a little hesitant, but I ordered the water buffalo and fried rice. To my surprise, it tasted just like beef.[6]

---

[5] *Ibid*, p.38.
[6] Personal communication with Jim Schneider on March 11, 2004.

Jim Schneider

I also remember a couple of trips into Dong Ha. On one occasion, Sam Baldon and I went to a Vietnamese tavern to have a few beers. We were sitting in the bar when a couple of ARVN (South Vietnamese) troops got upset because the waitress was spending too much time at our table, and I guess they felt she was ignoring them. They tried to pick a fight with us, but we did not back down. I knew that in a tight situation that I could count on Sam to back me up, and vice versa. At least one of them was armed with a .45 cal. pistol. Dino and I were not armed; nonetheless, we were not about to take anything off these guys. I don't remember who or what intervened, but the ARVN troops backed off. I especially remember this incident not because of the near fight, but rather because Sam and I had the opportunity to take a few moments out of the war just to sit back and enjoy a couple of beers together.

Bob Stemock surrounded by Vietnamese children

Dave Green recalled a chance meeting with an old Vietnamese man on the bridge crossing the Cua Viet River in Dong Ha. In Dave's own words:

> He was tall for a Vietnamese, walnut brown without a gram of fat, ancient lined face with obsidian eyes above teeth stained obsidian black from decades of beetle nut juice. His splayed toes seemed to grip the ground while thin, knotted legs disappeared into black silk pants rolled to mid thigh. A brown, split-bamboo coolie hat sat atop his head. A study in blacks and browns.
>
> We were center span of the Dong Ha Bridge, stretching north to south across the Dong Ha River on Highway One. I had seen him fishing from the bank far below. My choice was to go into the village of Dong Ha for warm bottles of Ba M'Ba, "33" Export Biere, followed by a blinding headache, or walk up to and out the bridge to vicariously enjoy my favorite past-time.
>
> Sure, the river was different, the fish were different, and the

bait was different, but the person behind the pole was the same—be it Galilee or Broken Bow, Oklahoma—a fisherman.

I've often thought that should Jesus return, I hope I'll meet him on a riverbank. I'll ask him if he prefers a Black Wooly-worm or a Royal Coachman for catching rainbow. He should know, after all he was a fisher of men.

The old man ignored me as I squatted on my heels, amazed at the contraption he was using and the skill with which he was using it. The line was wrapped around a can snaking through two guides attached to a bamboo pole. Holding the can in one hand and the pole in the other, he would sling the line and bait in a long graceful arc to the muddy water below. He controlled the speed of his cast by subtle tilts of the can. He made it look so easy when he did it, but I was convinced that, given a chance, I would have ended up with a ball of fishing line that would have made Gordian's look like a slipknot. I never saw him catch a fish, but that's never the point anyway, is it?

He was an artist, a master in one of life's oldest dances, and I the student. I never asked to try, he never offered.

But like a good master, he allowed me to watch, to learn, to remember.[7]

The bridge that Dave so aptly described above was blown up during the 1972 Easter Offensive to prevent North Vietnamese tanks from entering the village of Dong Ha. Nonetheless, the North Vietnamese Army eventually overran Dong Ha. There were no American military forces located at Dong Ha at the time. The Air Force and Marines had already abandoned the radar site and the Marine combat base, respectively.

When he got the opportunity, Sam Baldon liked to go into the

---

[7] Green, David M. "A Memory Dedicated to Mr. Phu Nguyen," *The Stubborn Twig,* Portland, Oregon, 1998. Used with permission.

village and take pictures of the town and the people. The picture below of a little Vietnamese girl from the village of Dong Ha represents the innocence of a nation that was torn by war.

Little Vietnamese girl in the village of Dong Ha

During the day, the children from the village would come up to the main gate at the base. We would give them candy and chewing gum. Like children everywhere, they seemed happy and carefree, but they were growing up in a country spilling over with death and destruction.

Joe Lee and Vietnamese children

49

We lived in tents, used field latrines, had no running or hot water for showers, and for awhile ate only C-rations until a makeshift chow hall was built. Though later we had hot meals, we still continued to eat C-rations at night when we were out on post.

Airmen cleaning mess kits

We were a very close-knit group. Our unit was small, which I think made us feel special. We were also located at a remote site and were assigned to a radar unit rather than an air police squadron. We had very little interaction with the other airmen on the site, thus we depended totally on each other. Our living conditions also forced us into close contact with one another.

On one of my trips into Dong Ha, I saw the body of a Viet Cong with half of his face blown away lying in the village square (I assume as a warning to the villagers not to aid the VC). One of the Bandits took a picture of the VC and distributed it to the rest of us. I kept this picture for many years and at some point decided to get rid of it, as it no longer seemed poignant to me. Like many Vietnam vets, I let go of the past, and that picture was simply something I didn't want to keep around anymore. However, I never forgot the Bandits.

Life was difficult for the American servicemen serving in Vietnam; however, at the end of a one-year tour of duty, we got to go home. For the Vietnamese people, the war would go on for another ten years.

Ole Doc Grover

A landmine killed our mascot, a dog-named "Bandit." Bandit had survived a previous encounter in the minefield. The "Doc" from the radar squadron patched him up; however, the second time he was not so fortunate. By the way, I called all the airmen from the 620th TCS "radar airmen." As Air Police assigned to a radar squadron, we were segregated, both physically and psychologically from the other airmen at Dong Ha. I did not recall Doc's name, but later (in 2003) found out that it was William Grover. It turned out that Doc was pretty much like us—not really a part of the radar squadron. The Bandits will forever remember Doc Grover for his kindhearted treatment of our dog. He saved Bandit's life once and did his best to do so a second time; however, Bandit was mortally wounded.

Doc was a member of the original crew that was assigned TDY to Dong Ha from Clark Air Base in the Philippines that helped set up the radar squadron at Dong Ha in November 1965. Doc's story of how he was assigned to Dong Ha can best be told in his own words:

My Dong Ha story begins in early October 1965 at Clark Air Force Base, Philippines. I was NCOIC of Central Sterile Supply at the hospital. My crew and I were responsible for cleaning, packing, and sterilizing all the instruments used in the hospital and at one point we were doing work for the field hospitals in Vietnam. With all the casualties we were getting plus the work we were doing for Nam, we didn't have much time for play.

The medical squadron received a request for a 7 Level NCO Medical Technician to go TDY to Nam for sixty days. Now

I know that there were at least twenty to thirty 7 Level NCOs assigned to that hospital at that time, but somehow I got that assignment. However, I didn't complain because I knew that for every one day I was in Nam, it counted as two days at Clark, and I had given up on getting my family there with me, so this was a way for me to get back with my family early.

I attended a briefing at Clark Air Force Base where I was told that I would be part of a group going to Vietnam to set up a radar station to control air traffic over North Vietnam. I was advised that I should take enough medical supplies for sixty days. After that briefing, it was about ten days before we left Clark. We stopped at Tan Son Nhut overnight. The reason I remembered this so well is the place they gave me to sleep was ankle deep in water with mosquitoes as big as horse flies, so I went back out on the runway and slept under the wing of the plane we had come in on and were going to leave on the next day.[1]

Sergeant Bradford was, and still is, a good ole boy from Alabama. He was able to find Doc Grover (apparently, Doc was another good ole boy from Alabama) and invited him to our second reunion at Branson, Missouri (July 2003). Below is an excerpt from Doc's recollection about the Bandits and our mascot, Bandit:

I have heard several stories on how they got the name "Bandits," but I will let them tell that, as they want it told. They somehow came up with a little brown dog as their mascot and they named him Bandit. There are several different stories on that too. Bandit got a little too far into the minefield one day and hit one of the trip wires causing some injuries to his back leg. Sgt. Bradford came up carrying

---

[1] Personal communication with Bill Grover on March 5, 2004.

Bandit in his arms. He wanted to know if Doc could do anything for Bandit. Now I could have said no, but if I did, I would have been a marked man with a target on my back for as long as I stayed on that site. So, I looked at Bandit. It turned out that Bandit came through his ordeal in pretty good shape. He had two flesh wounds and a broken leg. The flesh wounds I wasn't worried about. Being an ole southern boy with dogs around all my life, I knew they would heal up all right. The broken leg would also heal but if it weren't kept in good alignment the dog would limp for the rest of its life. Now, from the look on Sgt. Bradford's face and seeing the other guys with this little dog, I knew I had to play this one all the way out. So, I got busy cutting hair away from the wounds, cleaning them up real good and bandaging them. Then came the hard part. I could get the bones to line up good in the dog's leg but I couldn't figure out how to keep them there. Finally, I remembered an old splint set that came with some of the stuff I had ordered that no one used any more. There was some basil wood splints in the set that was easy to cut and work with, so I got a piece of that and shaped me up a splint for the dog's leg. When I was finished, I had a funny looking dog but a happy looking Sergeant. I told him someone would have to keep a close watch on the dog because he would chew the bandages off. I really don't believe the dog touched the ground for the next five or six weeks. When we took the bandages off, we had a good, healthy dog again. The sad part of this story is that the dog did not learn his lesson and was not as lucky the second time.[2]

---

[2] *Ibid*, Bill Grover.

Doc Grover, Sgt. Bradford, and Bandit

Based on information from a letter written by Sergeant Bradford to his wife, Bandit was killed when he ventured back into the minefield on February 27, 1966.

Doc Grover made some additional comments about our mascot Bandit and his relationship to the Bandits today:

> This story about the dog has had a very unusual effect on my life. First, it's why I am a part of the Bandit family. I took the time to do something for them when they needed my help. They were away from home, fighting in a war that no one believed in, yet doing what their country asked of them. We all found a bond with each other there and it still holds us together, even after these thirty-nine years. There were no parades or welcome home parties for us.
>
> The other thing the little dog story brings to mind is how other people see me. In twenty years of military service, all in the medical career field, I have pulled people out of crashed airplanes, from wrecked cars, and all kinds of accidents and family arguments, birthed seven babies,

sewn people back together from bar fights, and just about every thing else you can think of. Yet, I got more publicity from taking care of a little brown dog than any thing I ever did for a human being. That story was published in three state side papers and the *Stars and Stripes*. But no one really cared except for my brother Bandits.[3]

One of the papers that told of Doc's treatment of our mascot Bandit was a story about Dong Ha, published in *The Air Division Advisor*. TSgt. Charles Horne reported: "The 'Doc,' as he is fondly called recently set the broken bones of the site mascot, Bandit. The brown mongrel puppy wandered into the mine field and tripped off a mine. Now five months old, the puppy is doing well— and staying out of the mine field."[4]

Doc did something for us when someone else might not have. He was the medical technician for the radar site; what he did for Bandit, he did for us. And his act of kindness in treating Bandit will never be forgotten. Perhaps a lesson from this story is that you never know when a small act of compassion will make a difference—not only in your life but also in the lives of many other people. Doc could have said no, that treating a mongrel puppy was not in his job requirements, but the fact that he didn't speaks volumes about his character.

Sergeant Bradford summed up the feelings the Bandits had for this little dog:

> One of my saddest memories was on the day our mascot Bandit was killed in the minefield. That little dog had meant so much to the Bandits. Bandit was like one of us. He was a reminder of a little piece of home in this desolate war-torn country. Doc Grover had patched him up after his first trip into the minefield, but he couldn't save him this time.[5]

[3] *Ibid*, Bill Grover.
[4] Horne, TSgt. Charles E. "Airmen Defend Lonely Radar Site: They Call It Little Alamo." *The Air Division Advisor*, 2 (8), March 4, 1966, pp. 1, 4.
[5] Bradford, Carl L. "A Message to My Troops: Defenders of Dong Ha Air Base, Republic of Vietnam 1956-1966." *Tiger Flight, 13* (3) 2004, pp. 37-41.

Ed Cheri, Sgt. Bradford, Sam Baldon, Jack Case, and Bandit

In the following passage, Ed Cheri echoes Sergeant Bradford's sentiments and adds his memories of Bandit and Doc's treatment of Bandit after his encounters in the minefield:

> I can't forget our mascot, Bandit. He brought a lot of fun and much laughter to our life at Dong Ha. I know we got Bandit out of the village; I don't remember how, but I think we stole him. Bandit was just a puppy and as far as we were concerned, if we didn't take him, he would end up in some one's pot when he got bigger. Bandit ended up going out into the minefield, where we had six rows of M16A1s, Bouncing Bettys, both trip and pressure. He was injured badly. He managed to crawl out of the field without setting off any more mines. He was taken to Doc, our medic and he worked wonders on him, sewed him up and splintered his hind leg. After that, every time the big guns went off, Bandit would run like hell for a bunker. Some time passed and he saw he wasn't getting hurt, and unfortunately, he wandered back into the minefield and was killed. That was a very sad day for all.[6]

---

[6] Personal communication with Ed Cheri on February 28, 2004.

Ed's recollection of how we acquired Bandit from the village of Dong Ha seems quite appropriate, given our nickname "Bandits," and it seems only fitting that he should be called Bandit. After all these years, no one is really sure who stole this little puppy and brought him back to our camp. Some say it was Jack Case and others say it was Ed Cheri. Most likely it could have been either one, either singly or together, or it could have been someone else. Jack and Ed were very close friends and where you saw one, you usually saw the other. I suppose it really does not matter who took the puppy because what we did at Dong Ha, we did as a group, and we saw an act by one as an act by all.

Jim Schneider and Bandit

Jim Schneider had the following to say about Bandit:

> Jack Case and another air policeman rescued (though some might call it stealing) a little puppy from the village and brought him back to our tent. We named him Bandit. Not long after we got him, I heard an explosion out in the minefield. It was Bandit. He had apparently set off one of the trip mines and was hurt. I don't know how we got him out of the minefield, but somehow we did. The Doc (Bill Grover)

fixed his back leg that had been injured in the explosion. We had a hard time trying to keep the bandages on Bandit, but he survived. However, Bandit went back into the minefield on another occasion and was killed.[7]

Doc Grover had been at Dong Ha for about four and half months. He was responsible for providing medical care to about 150 airmen that were now assigned to the base. However, Doc was one of the old-timers at Dong Ha. He had come up with the original crew of airmen from the 620th TCS that had been assigned to Dong Ha to set up the site. Doc recalled that first night and the his first few days at Dong Ha:

> I was on the first plane that landed. We landed on a dirt runway. There were no buildings, nothing, and it was raining. Looking after my supplies and trying to keep up with things, it didn't take long to get wet. I stayed wet for about four days. After all our equipment was on the ground and the planes gone we had the task of moving every thing over the top of the next little hill where we would establish our permanent base. That first night, there were only about twenty-five to thirty of us there. We had been told that a detachment of Marines would meet us there for security purposes, but they never showed up. So here we were, wet, tired, and hungry. C-rations tasted pretty good that first night and several nights after that too. Was I scared that first night? Sure I was and most nights after that also, but we did what good soldiers do, we made the best of what we had. The next day more supplies came in but not any more men. Our objective was to build a radar site and get it operational and that took first priority. I don't remember how many days it took but it was only two or three days when the radar unit went into service. It was still raining and I was still wet, however no one had gotten hurt and the VC had left us alone. As time went by things got better. We got in some tents

---

[7] Personal communication with Jim Schneider on March 11, 2004.
[8] Personal communication with Bill Grover on March 5, 2004.

58

and it quit raining. As plywood became available, we put floors in the tents. My tent was set up with all my medical equipment in the front half and my living quarters in the back half so I was in pretty good shape.[8]

Doc stated that there were no security personnel at Dong Ha when he first arrived; however, he remembered an air policeman by the name of Sergeant Burton showing up later. I believe the sergeant he referred to was from Na Trang Air Base and was in charge of eight air policemen—four from Na Trang and four more from Tan Son Nhut. They were the group of air police that were assigned TDY (Temporary Duty) to Dong Ha that we replaced.

Doc had an interesting story about how he managed to get the medical supplies he needed:

I was told I would be gone for sixty days and should only carry medical supplies for that time. However, I was there well over sixty days and had about 150 personnel I was responsible for. I was running low on medical supplies. I had ordered supplies twice through regular channels and had received nothing. I went to Major Cummings and told him I wanted to call the Colonel that briefed us back in the Philippines, he said okay. I told the Colonel what my problem was and what I had done to try to correct it. He asked me if I had a list of supplies that I needed. The next day a plane came in and one of the airmen from the site came over and got me. He said the loadmaster on the plane had some supplies that he would not release to anyone but me. The loadmaster, a Tech. Sergeant, told me to be sure to tell the Colonel that he got my supplies to me. He said the Colonel told him that if he didn't deliver the supplies, he might as well not come back to Clark Air Force Base again, because when he left that time he would not be a Tech. Sergeant.[9]

---

[9] *Ibid,* Bill Grover.

Later on, a second medical technician by the name of Staff Sergeant Wheeler was assigned to Dong Ha to help out Doc Grover. Doc also found time to treat some of the Vietnamese villagers for a various illnesses, ailments, and so on. Doc described a visit by a Vietnamese girl about twenty years old and her parents that was out of the ordinary. Apparently the girl came to see Doc complaining about having a stomachache. When Doc examined her, he discovered that the girl was pregnant. Doc Wheeler confirmed his diagnosis. A Vietnamese interpreter communicated the news of the daughter's condition to the parents and the girl. It seems that this was not the sort of information they wanted to hear and Doc soon had a family crisis on his hands. Doc tried to explain the medical situation to them, but it was evident that they did not want to accept the truth. Finally, Doc had to ask them to leave so he and Doc Wheeler could see other patients. They returned about thirty minutes later and the father asked Doc to perform an abortion—something neither Doc Grover nor Doc Wheeler was about to do. They had the family escorted off base and gave orders that they were not to be allowed back on the site.

Doc Grover's sixty day TDY tour at Dong Ha, which had been extended to five and a half months, was coming to a close. He was assigned to MacDill Air Force Base, Florida. Doc would later return to Vietnam where he served with the 558th Medical Services Flight at Vinh Long. He was a member of a small team of medical technicians and doctors who treated Vietnamese civilian war casualties. For his meritorious service at Vinh Long, he was awarded the Air Force Commendation Medal.[10]

---

[10] Personal communication with Bill Grover on January 31, 2006.

Sergeant Bradford's Leaving

No single event marks the transition for the Bandits more than when our leader, TSgt. Carl Bradford, received his orders to go back to the States after serving his one-year tour in Vietnam. Sergeant Bradford was the first to go home, leaving Dong Ha on March 27, 1966. He had trained us well and his influence was with us until the last Bandit left Dong Ha. His first priority was that all of his troops would safely return home. He took care of us and we respected him and we would have done anything for him. There is always risk in war, but Sergeant Bradford did not needlessly put his troops in danger. Nonetheless, we were all prepared to give our lives, if need be, in the defense of one another and Dong Ha.

The day before he left, we had a formal change-of-command between TSgt. Bradford and SSgt. Hester. It was probably the only guardmount we had while Sergeant Bradford was the NCOIC. We usually met with Sarge in his tent or, if he had an individual assignment, he talked with the person directly. However, his replacement, Staff Sergeant Robert C. Hester, came directly to Dong Ha from a stateside base and under his "command," or lack thereof, things began to change for the worse at Dong Ha. I will have more to say about Hester later in the chapter, none of it complimentary. For as much as Sergeant Bradford was liked and respected by the Bandits, Hester was disliked—and for some that would be putting it mildly.

Change of command

Before Sarge left, we gave him one hell of a going-away party—the biggest party for anyone during our tour at Dong Ha. All of the Bandits, the new Air Police replacements, the Marines who had come up to Dong Ha to work with us, and the site commander, Major Cummings were present.

Our "renegade" reputation at Dong Ha was well deserved. With the exception of a few encounters with the other airmen on the base, we pretty much stuck to ourselves. We were "cops" and we didn't really feel welcomed by the radar squadron. From the beginning, we took an "us" versus "them" attitude, and it was evidently mutual. However, a platoon of Marines from Kilo Company, Third Battalion/Fourth Marines had just arrived at Dong Ha and we invited them to our party. We got along better and had more in common with the Marines than we did with the radar airmen. We were the ones out on the perimeter safeguarding the camp so the airmen could sleep without worrying about Charlie. The VC were not going to get through the wire on our watch. Like the Marines, we took pride in being "grunts" and we were prepared to give our lives defending that little piece of dirt called Dong Ha.

Someone took a picture of Ed Cheri and Jack Case holding each other up during the party. As Sarge would have most likely said, "they're a bunch of damn Bandits."

Ed Cheri and Jack Case

Sarge had almost completed his tour of duty in Vietnam and was going home. The party was a tribute to him and what he had done for his troops at Dong Ha. The party was our way of showing him just how much we appreciated him as a leader. He would be sorely missed, yet we were happy for him.

The next morning, Sergeant Bradford got out of a jeep on the airstrip at Dong Ha. He would soon be on his way back to the world and, eventually, to his wife and children in Alabama.

TSgt. Bradford on the airstrip

Sarge said his goodbyes to those who had gathered to see him off. We were a little worn-out after the big "party" the day before. Remember, we also had to go out on post that night, so none of us had had any sleep. But Sarge's leaving was a big Bandit event and we were all there to put him on the plane. The Bandits were about to lose the best Sergeant in the whole damn Air Force.

Just before Sarge got on the plane, Dave Green handed him an envelope and asked him not to read it until he was out of Vietnam. Dave, in his own creative style, had composed a poem that put into words the feelings that all the Bandits felt for our leader, TSgt. Carl Bradford, both then and now.

This is the note Dave Green gave to Sarge when he left Dong Ha on March 27, 1966:[1]

A Toast to Ole Brad

Here's to ole Brad,
May his memory live,
In the hearts of the men,
To whom he did give,
His daily devotion,
His time and his best,
To make "Bradford's Bandits,"
Only the best.

Here's to the man,
Who always will be,
A well nurtured memory,
O'er life's troubled sea,
For always he taught us,
That we could best win,
Life's hardest battles,
If you face them like men.

Bradford, we'll miss you,
Cause we did depend,

[1] Bradford, Carl L. "A Message to My Troops: Defenders of Don Ha Air Base, Republic of Vietnam, 1956-1966." *Tiger Flight, 13* (3) 2004, pp. 37-41.

On you to lead us,
Through thick and through thin,
So Bandits for all.
And the rest, Go to Hell,
Goodbye! You Old Bastard;
We bid, FARE THEE WELL![2]

Some thirty-eight years later, this is what Sarge had to say:

I kept this poem with me along with other memorabilia from
my tour at Dong Ha. Throughout all the years since, I never
forgot my Bandits. My time with these young men had a
profound effect on my life from that time to the present. We
were close as brothers, and in fact we are brothers. Each one
is special to me and I still love my Bandits.[3]

Putting Sarge on the plane

The Bandits and the new troops who had come up to Dong Ha
in February and March jumped into the back of a 5-ton truck and
drove to the edge of the airstrip to see Sarge's plane take off.

---

[2] Green, David M. "A Toast to Ole Brad," unpublished poem, March 27, 1966.
[3] Bradford, "A Message to My Troops," p. 41.

Bandits on the end of the runway

Just a few weeks later, a security officer from the radar unit became more involved in our operations. One night, Lieutenant Richard and SSgt. Hester (our new NCOIC) came to my M-60 post (manned with John Bertolet) along the south berm. The Lieutenant ordered me to crawl out to the barbed wire fence in front of the minefield and then crawl halfway between two M-60 machine gun bunkers. Before I went over the berm, I asked him if the other posts had been notified that I would be out there. He said yes. The alleged purpose of this mission was to set up a listening post halfway between the two M-60 bunkers. Unbeknownst to me, as I was crawling along the edge of the minefield, Dave Green had his finger on the trigger of an M-60 machine gun ready to open fire. Lee, who was manning the M-60 with Green, called in to the command post and only then was told that I was out there. Lee said, "That's a good way to get somebody killed," to which the lieutenant responded, "That was what we were here for." At Dong Ha in 1966, we did not have to call into CSC (Central Security Control) to get permission to fire. If something or someone was in the wire, it was not supposed to be there—except in my case. One can only imagine what an M-60 would have done to my body at that range. Thank goodness, we were not in the practice of engaging in a free-fire zone whenever someone popped a hand flare. Some military units in

Vietnam opened fire at the slightest noise or movement along the wire. I can recall numerous times when water buffaloes and dogs were detected near the perimeter fence.

Needless to say, I did not have much respect for that Lieutenant after this incident. I am here today because Lee and Green followed their instincts and did not fire. I owe them my life— they should have fired but I am thankful they didn't. I can only wonder if the situation was reversed, would Bertolet and I have opened fire on either Joe or Dave?

Dave Green, some 38 years later, was a bit more succinct in his account of the incident:

> Bill Bland is alive today for no other reason than Joe Lee and
> I didn't kill him when he crawled in front of our gun slit at
> two in the morning. I'm still not sure why he's alive; he just
> seemed a little bit too big to be a V.C. I cannot imagine the
> terror that went through Bill's mind when the slide went
> forward on our M-60 machine gun and he realized that he
> was a dead man.[4]

I recall that someone sent up a slap-flare lighting up the area for about thirty seconds. During that time I was exposed out in the open, but I was not aware that Joe and Dave were taking a bead on me. I had been told by the Lieutenant that the other posts would be notified that I was out there. The fact was that the Lt. hadn't told anyone.

Lieutenant Richard had the nickname "Cowboy" at Dong Ha; however, he was not very well liked by the Bandits. Certainly for me, after the incident above, I had little or no respect for him as an officer or as a man. Similarly, I had no respect for SSgt. Hester for the same reasons. He was supposedly one of us—but he was never a Bandit.

SSgt. Hester never had the respect the Bandits had for Sergeant Bradford. Respect is earned, not given to someone because of rank or position. Bradford was a leader of men; Hester was simply the NCO who had been placed in charge by higher-ups. He attempted to run operations as if we were on a safe, secure

---

[4] Personal communication with Dave Green on July 19, 2002.

stateside base. Hester was a by-the-books regulations type of individual. He was also fond of inspections at guardmount before we went out on post. Right after he took over as the NCOIC, he asked me why my boots were not polished. After four months of working in the rain and mud, all of the polish had worn off and my "black" boots had turned almost white. I put some polish on my boots; however, I was not about to spit-shine them. In the field conditions where we lived and worked, we may have been dirty and muddy—but our weapons were clean. Hester never truly commanded the unit. In my opinion, he did not have the backbone to stand up to the security officer (Lt. Richard) from the radar squadron.

Things were never the same after Sergeant Bradford left. We did our job, but not with the same enthusiasm as before. I think we were all just putting in our time before we got to go home. Dong Ha was still a dangerous place, but we did not have much confidence in SSgt. Hester. The Bandits relied upon the leadership of A1Cs Case, Cheri, and Stemock to actually run the unit. We had been in combat together and knew that we could count on these men to protect our backs.

Tech Sergeant Bradford was a lean, mean, fighting machine in 1966. Thirty-six years later, at our first reunion after the war, we found out just how softhearted Sarge really was. We did not see that side of him at Dong Ha. In Vietnam, he had a job to do and he did it like a professional soldier. For that, we respected him. Today, we have the privilege of knowing the whole man. He is still our Bandit leader, but most of all he is our friend and our brother.

While we were in Vietnam, we knew very little about Sergeant Bradford's personal life. We may have assumed that he was married and had children, but that was not something discussed. The rest of us were single and our perspective on being away from home was entirely different. Young and perhaps a little arrogant, we viewed the war as an adventure. No one actually thought he would be killed, but there is nothing like the adrenaline rush of being in combat. We had just enough combat experience to make us feel invincible.

Further, in the Air Force and in other branches of the military,

NCOs and airmen were not allowed to fraternize. Informal norms would also have prohibited such socialization patterns between individuals of different rank. Sergeant Bradford was our leader, not our best buddy in Vietnam. Our relationship was based on respect and we looked up to Sarge. Today we have quite a different relationship with him and can share our personal stories and lives together. That would not have been practical or possible while we were serving in the military.

Since that first reunion, we have been able to piece together a brief biography of his life and military career prior to 1965. Carl L. Bradford was born in a cotton mill village near Huntsville, Alabama on December 28, 1932. He was the seventh child in a large family of ten children. He had four brothers and five sisters. Though he grew up during the Depression, he was blessed with a wonderful, close-knit family, that stuck together in both good times and bad. Carl's father died as the result of an accident at work in 1944, leaving six children at home. His mother went to work in the cotton mill and his older sister Judy took over at home, caring for the family. Carl's mom lived in their village home until 1992, when she passed away.

In 1948, at the age of fifteen, Carl joined the Alabama Army National Guard. In 1950, his unit was activated for duty during the Korean War. Within a few days, he was on his way to Fort Campbell, Kentucky, for training. His unit was headed for Korea. However, when the Army discovered that he was only seventeen years old, Carl was discharged. He returned to high school, and upon graduation decided to join the Air Force.

On February 7, 1952, Carl Bradford enlisted in the U.S. Air Force. After eight weeks of basic training at Lackland AFB, Texas, he went to Supply Tech School at Francis E. Warren AFB, Wyoming. Upon completion of tech school, he was assigned to Laredo AFB, Texas. In April 1954, he was assigned to Kunsan, Korea, and later reassigned to Tachikawa AFB, Japan. He remained there for the rest of his enlistment, until being discharged in December 1955.

It was during this time at home that Carl met and later married Elizabeth. He reenlisted in the Air Force for six years on March 12, 1956 and was stationed at MacDill AFB, Florida. From there he went TDY (temporary duty) to Morocco, North Africa. After returning from North Africa, he was assigned to Brize Norton RAF Base, England. His two oldest sons Michael and Mark were born in England. Next, he was assigned to Biggs AFB, Texas. His youngest son, Brett, was born in El Paso.

Carl had made Staff Sergeant in three years, eleven months in his first enlistment, but could not get promoted to Tech Sergeant in six years on his second enlistment. During those years, Sarge said it was almost impossible to get promoted because of the large number of NCOs who stayed in the Air Force following the Korean War. Thus, he decided to leave the Air Force a second time, in 1962.

Carl worked for a brief period as a police officer with the Huntsville Police Department. Though he enjoyed working as a policeman, he missed the Air Force. His wife Elizabeth loved the military life too and would say to Carl "I wish we were still in the Air Force." Carl reenlisted and requested to be cross-trained into the Air Police. He was assigned to the 341st Combat Defense Squadron, Malmstrom AFB, Montana. In July 1963, his only daughter Kelly was born. He was promoted to Tech. Sergeant in 1964. At Malmstrom, he worked Security, Investigations, and later became the NCOIC of Law Enforcement.

TSgt. Bradford received his orders for Vietnam and arrived at Tan Son Nhut Air Base in April 1965. Several months later, in December, the Bandits met him for the first time, just before we left for Dong Ha. We knew nothing about his life or his family. We would not find out these things about him until thirty-six years later, at our first reunion after the war.

VC and NVA Activity

In April 1966, we were completely surrounded by VC and NVA (North Vietnamese Army) of approximately fifteen hundred total enemy troops. In addition, the ARVN 1st Division, located in Hue, forty miles south of us, assigned to defend the province, was in sympathy with the Buddhist protests that had begun in March. There was talk of a possible military coup; thus we were facing South Vietnamese troops as well.

At one point, several ARVN (Army of Republic of Vietnam) soldiers fired their weapons into the air in a symbolic gesture of aggression. We countered by firing a short burst from our M-16s into the air. We were not afraid of the VC or NVA and we were certainly not afraid of the South Vietnamese troops. We were nonetheless, as much concerned about facing off with the ARVN troops as we were the VC. Interestingly, at Dong Ha, the Vietnamese referred to the Viet Cong as Viet Minh. That name seemed significant because the Vietnamese who had fought against the French under Ho Chi Minh were called Viet Minh.

All of the U.S. Army advisors from Quang Tri and nearby areas were evacuated, and we had several contingency evacuation plans. The base was rigged to blow if we left. Of course, APs would have been the last to leave.

The North Vietnamese slogan at the time was "Blood in April, Peace in May." We were obviously concerned that the NVA would drive down the DMZ in an attempt to occupy I Corps. This is exactly what happened in the 1972 Easter Offensive. By that time, I believe the Air Force had left Dong Ha. South Vietnamese Marines along with American Marine advisors defended the area. Quang Tri was destroyed and Dong Ha was overrun before South Vietnamese units and the small number of American combat forces still in-country at the time could halt the invasion.

Air Police Command Post

In a letter written April 7, 1966, John Bertolet enclosed the following news clipping about the upheaval in the government that was happening at the time. In the margin, he wrote that General Ky[1] "had the mayor of Da Nang shot." The newspaper article read:

Da Nang, Vietnam (UPI).

More than 300 pedicab cyclists and bus drivers paraded through the streets of Da Nang Monday in a demonstration against the Republic of Vietnam's ruling military government. The pedicabs and 3-wheeled buses were plastered with placards demanding a return to civilian government in Vietnam.

The 2-hour demonstration was an orderly one, with policemen directing traffic around the parade route. Da Nang has been the scene of several demonstrations in the past two weeks demanding the reinstatement of Lt. Gen. Nguyen

[1] Nguyen Cao Ky, the VNAF (Vietnamese Air Force) Commander had become Prime Minister of South Vietnam in June 1965.

72

Chanh Thi, who was fired as military commander of the five northern provinces.

In a letter home, John Bertolet wrote:

> The political situation in Da Nang also posed a threat to Dong Ha because the leader of the protest was a South Vietnamese Army General at Quang Tri, just east of us. His brother-in-law was the Army Colonel at Dong Ha. The situation was uncertain for a while. We did not know if he would turn his army against us or remain loyal to the military government. Besides keeping an eye out for the VC, we also had to watch the South Vietnamese army. There were several small groups and one large group of VC in the area and they seemed to be coming our way. In the event of a military coup, we had an evacuation plan set up.[2]

Jim Schneider had also saved a newspaper clipping that described some of the NVA activity that was occurring around Dong Ha in April 1966.[3] In two days of heavy fighting, approximately three to six thousand soldiers from the South Vietnamese Army's 1st Infantry Division engaged two battalions of NVA/VC (about one thousand men). The battle took place about halfway between Dong Ha and Quang Tri, and an estimated three hundred communist troops were killed, while South Vietnamese casualties were described as "light."

The article also mentioned the "recent political crisis in March," stating that some of the troops from the 1st Infantry Division had fought with Buddhist dissidents against the South Vietnamese central government in Da Nang and Hue in March of 1966.

Schneider had also kept a *Stars and Stripes* article describing the first major attack on Tan Son Nhut Air Base. This story was of interest to all of us because we had been stationed at TSN before coming up to Dong Ha. Also, one of our Bandits, Dave

---

[2] Bertolet, John A. "Letters Home from Vietnam." *Tiger Flight, 13,* (4), 2004, pp. 37-41.
[3] Saigon, Associated Press. "Viets Kill 300 Reds near DMZ," circa April 1966.

Green, was on R&R (rest and relaxation) in Saigon at the time.

According to the report,[4] Tan Son Nhut received seventy-five rounds of 81mm mortar and 75mm recoilless rifle fire. Seven U.S. servicemen were killed and 114 airmen were wounded. The main targets included the fuel storage area and aircraft parking areas; however, the main tower was hit and knocked out of commission. Most of the casualties were from rounds fired into the barracks areas.

The attack came from an area between the villages of Tan Son Nhut and Phu Tho Hoa—an area patrolled by Air Police security forces. The attack was launched from outside the base security perimeter. Tan Son Nhut was a large air base; those of us who had patrolled that same area when we were there were not at all surprised that the attack would have come from that location.

We were all thankful, of course, that Dave had survived the attack to rejoin us at Dong Ha. However, his R&R had been interrupted by having to pull security during two out of the three days he was in Saigon.

With the increased VC and NVA activity around Dong Ha, we had several incidents of sniper fire on the base. We were damn lucky that no one was ever hit. John Bertolet reported being fired upon on a couple of occasions while out at the firing range just off base.[5] Apparently, the VC were not willing to come in close enough to get off a really good shot. And we were just darn lucky that no one was ever hit. I remember that the latrine was a favorite target. Because it was slightly elevated, it actually stood above the berm line, making it a good target.

The Russian-made AK-47 was an ideal weapon for close-quarter fighting, particularly in a jungle environment. Due to the generous tolerances in manufacturing the AK-47, it would continue to fire even if it was dropped in the sand or mud—conditions that would jam an M-16. It had fairly good accuracy out to about a hundred meters, but it lacked the long-range accuracy of an M-16 rifle.

In my opinion, the sniper fire was directed more at harassing us than inflicting casualties. I think they just squeezed off a few rounds every now and then to let us know they were around.

[4] Baker, John K. "VC Hit Air Base Expertly." *Stars and Stripes,* circa April 1966.
[5] Bertolet, "Letters Home from Vietnam," p. 41.

On stateside bases, Air Police were authorized to use lethal force; however, we had a very strict policy on when we could fire. We always carried loaded weapons but an NCO had to supervise the loading and unloading of weapons at the beginning and end of each shift change. Even on bases like Tan Son Nhut, air police had to check out and turn in their weapons at an armory, NCOs supervised loading and unloading, and APs had to get permission from Central Security Control (CSC) to fire their weapons. This policy certainly didn't make sense—especially at a place like Dong Ha in the middle of a war zone where people were shooting at you.

Jack Case showing off some of our weapons

We kept our weapons with us, if for no other reason than we did not have an armory. We were allowed to lock and load and fire when the situation warranted. This policy continued even after Sergeant Bradford left. There was never a single incidence of an accidental firing and I don't know of any instance where an air policeman fired his weapon without good cause. We were in a combat zone. The restrictive firing policies that Air Police units on the much larger bases were under did not fit the situation at Dong Ha. If someone fired at you, it did not make sense to ask permission to fire back.

On one occasion, Jack Case fired a 40mm. round from an M-79 grenade launcher at a sniper location. No one knows if he hit the sniper but there was a trail of fresh blood in the area. The sniper fire ceased, at least for a while.

Though the M-16 was a more accurate rifle than the AK-47, it was prone to jamming if not cleaned properly; thus, we cleaned our weapons before we did anything else. We knew that our lives depended on keeping our weapons clean.

Although we would occasionally receive sniper fire during the day, all the previous mortar attacks had occurred at night. In late May 1966, however, I remember being awakened during the day by a round exploding just outside the east perimeter. Our tent was located on that side of the compound. I jumped out of my cot, put on my boots, ammo belt, flack jacket, helmet, and grabbed my M-16 and hit the berm in only my boxer shorts.

Vietnam's climate consists of two seasons: rainy and dry. We had arrived at Dong Ha during the rainy season. During January and February, it was cold! Vietnam was supposed to be a country with a warm climate; at least that is what I thought prior to going to Dong Ha. Thus, the only jacket I had was a light field jacket.

South Vietnam has two major monsoon seasons. In the south around Saigon, the season usually lasts between May and September. Most of us were at Tan Son Nhut during at least part of the rainy season. The monsoon season in the North starts in November and ends in March.

John Bertolet said: "The temperature at night was only in the 60s, but it seemed a lot colder."[6] Further, when we came off post in the morning, we were wet and muddy. The only way we had to clean up was a field shower. However, it really didn't matter because by that evening we went back out and got muddy all over again.

By April, the monsoon season had ended and the climate changed dramatically. Bertolet stated: "It was extremely hot by the end of April. It was 116 degrees in the sun and 100 degrees in the shade."[7] Not only was it hot, but after the rainy season was over, the camp became rather dusty. Bert wrote home: "The weather was terrible in early May. It got up over 105 degrees everyday and the wind made it a steady dust storm. But I only had 63 days left, so I didn't mind."[8]

[6] Bertolet, "Letters Home from Vietnam," p. 39.
[7] *Ibid*, p. 41.

By the middle of July, most of the original Bandits had rotated back to the States; however, Bob Stemock and Ed Cheri were still at Dong Ha when Operation Hastings began. This was the beginning of the large buildup of Marines in the area around Dong Ha.

Ed Cheri recalled observing firefights occurring within two miles of the perimeter, while fighter aircraft dropped bombs right off the airstrip in support of the ground troops. Ed also stated that an air police Tech Sergeant (name unknown) had been assigned to the unit around this time. According to Cheri, the new NCOIC brought organization to the unit; something that Staff Sergeant Hester had not been able to do.

During the period of May 18-26, 1966, U.S. and South Vietnamese troops entered the DMZ for the first time. I remember a Marine artillery unit that was located just off the west end of the airstrip at about this time. I believe they were there for about a week. I don't remember them being at Dong Ha when I left in the middle of June.

Bob Stemock recalled that in either July or August 1966, a battalion of North Vietnamese Regulars were right outside the base perimeter, at the east end of the airstrip. Bob stated:

> Major Cummings ordered that we were not to fire at them unless fired upon first. He wanted us all alive in the morning and not a bunch of dead heroes. During most of the night, we could hear the NVA talking and their canteens and rifles clanging as they crossed the end of the runway. Fortunately, there was not an incident.[9]

On July 15, 1966, Operation Hastings kicked off. During this operation, U.S. Marines and South Vietnamese troops engaged ten thousand NVA in Quang Tri Province. This action was the largest combined military operation to date in the war. On July 30, 1966, the United States began bombing the NVA in the DMZ.

---

[8] *Ibid*, p. 41.

[9] Personal communication with Bob Stemock on March 12, 2004.

Our Heroes

The big attack did not come while we were at Dong Ha; however, we had a number of casualties. During our tour, nine airmen lost their lives as a result of combat action or were killed in the line of duty. Six were killed in an enemy ambush, two were killed in a vehicle crash (one was an AP named Joseph Packer), and a Forward Air Controller (OE-1 pilot) was killed in a mid-air collision with a Marine helicopter. They are our heroes. One of our own, Ed Cheri, was seriously injured in a minefield explosion. Later in the war, another Bandit, Jack Case (then U.S. Army Ranger), was captured by the enemy and spent nineteen months in a POW camp before being released.

On June 5, 1966, six airmen were killed in a VC ambush near Dong Ha. They were on a surveying mission for the SAC (Strategic Air Command) "Sky Spot" unit that would later be assigned to Dong Ha. As far as I know, they never requested a police escort. I am sure if they had, we would have gone with them. The airmen were armed with M-16 rifles, however they were ambushed before they could get off a shot. I don't know if it would have made a difference, but as Air Police, we would have been armed with M-60 machine guns. Perhaps we could have secured their flank, thus allowing them to focus on their mission. While I have read accounts that differ, my understanding was that Marines from Phu Bai, on a recon patrol, found their burned-out vehicle and returned the bodies to Dong Ha. I do recollect walking past the temporary morgue (tent) that housed the bodies before they were shipped out.

Also, on June 16, 1966, two airmen were killed in a vehicle accident while returning from a trip to Quang Tri. Their names were A2C Joseph E. Packer, Jr. and SMSgt. (Senior Master Sergeant) Russell J. Sisley. Packer was an Air Policeman and was driving the vehicle. SMSgt. Sisley was a radar technician with the unit (Det. 1, 620th TCS). Airman Packer had arrived at Dong Ha sometime around the middle of March while SMSgt. Sisley had been assigned to the site in January 1966. While their deaths were reported as an accident (non-combat), the vehicle in which they were riding may have come under fire causing Airman Packer to lose control of the vehicle. The area was well known as "sniper alley." The vehicle overturned and landed upside down in the water near a small, wood planked bridge on Highway 1. In addition to the two Americans killed, an ARVN interpreter assigned to Dong Ha AB was injured.

Joseph Packer, unidentified AP, and Ed Cheri

When word of the crash reached Dong Ha, all available Air Police grabbed their weapons and jumped into the back of a truck to go to their aid. Jim Schneider was one of the first to respond, and drove us toward the site of the crash. I am not positive, but I believe we got only as far as the end of the dirt airstrip when we saw the bodies being brought back to Dong Ha.

Although the Air Force designated the crash as an accident, we were told at the time that the convoy was attacked. Jim Schneider said:

> I remember it was late afternoon, and we were filling sandbags when we got word that there was an accident involving one of our Air Policemen. I drove the truck

carrying some other Air Policemen to the site of the accident. Airman Packer drove off the side of a bridge and landed on a riverbank below. He was killed instantly. I don't recall what happened after we arrived at the accident site. A few days after this incident, I left Dong Ha to go home.[1]

Ed Cheri was on R&R at the time of the accident, but he remembered the wooden bridge on Highway 1 between Dong Ha and Quang Tri. Ed said:

I hated that bridge. It was narrow and had two planks down the center. Every time I would drive across it I would take my time because it was very slick and if you didn't hit it just right you could lose control. I think that was what happened to Airman Packer.[2]

The mangled weapons carrier was brought back to the Dong Ha radar site.

Wrecked weapons carrier

Bertolet, Schneider, and myself had only a few days left at Dong Ha when Packer was killed. However, not one of us hesitated in going on this mission. I do remember thinking how

[1] Personal communication with Jim Schneider on March 11, 2004.
[2] Personal communication with Ed Cheri on February 28, 2004.

short (time left in-country) I was at that moment, but it was only a passing thought.

Packer was one of our own, but we never had the opportunity to mourn his death. He was only twenty years old when he died. Our tour was up and we were going home. We were the lucky ones. Airman Packer and SMSgt. Sisley and so many others would be leaving Vietnam in body bags. They were the real heroes of the Vietnam War. "All gave some, some gave all" is an appropriate way to describe the sacrifice that they made for our country. Our hearts go out to the families of Airman Packer and SMsgt. Sisley and to all the families who lost loved ones during the war.

On July 23, 1966, Air Force Captain William Ward Smith, a Forward Air Controller, was controlling a flight of F-4B fighter aircraft in support of U.S. Marines in Operation Hastings in Quang Tri Province. After successfully directing the air strikes, his O-1E aircraft collided in mid-air with a Marine helicopter. Air Force para-rescue forces spotted his body but, because of the heavy hostile activity on the ground, were not able to recover Captain Smith's remains. He had arrived in Vietnam on May 26, 1966. Captain Smith was awarded the Silver Star and Purple Heart[3] posthumously.[4]

I would like to mention the heroism of several members of our unit. A1C Ed Cheri and A1C Bob Stemock were laying a minefield along the north perimeter of the site separating the Air Force compound from the ARVN compound. They had already laid the tangle foot (strands of barbwire) and several rows of mines. Cheri stated that one of the mines went off, throwing him backwards, and he landed near where Bob was laying his mines.[5]

Extremely fortunate for Ed, he landed on the tangle foot, which prevented other mines from going off. He said he did not feel any pain; however, he could hear himself screaming—though he said it sounded like someone falling off a cliff miles away. Then, according to Ed, Bob cleared a path in the minefield to get him out. In addition, a medic from the unit had climbed into the

---

[3] The Silver Star is awarded for gallantry in action against an enemy of the United States while engaged in military operations. The Purple Heart is awarded for wounds received in combat action while serving with the armed forces of the United States.

[4] Information on Captain Smith was retrieved March 5, 2004 from http://www.virtualwall.org.

[5] Personal communication with Ed Cheri on February 28, 2004.

minefield and was trying to stop the bleeding. A Navy doctor was also present and attended to him once he was out of the minefield. The explosion had severely injured his legs, chest, and arms (approximately twenty-six total wounds). He was taken to the Marine compound at Dong Ha, where a chaplain gave him last rights. Ed further commented that there was an U.S. Air Force plane on the runway, but they refused to transport him because they did not have a medic on board. Instead, he was med-evacced out of Dong Ha on September 11, 1966 on a Marine Corps helicopter to Phu Bai, a Marine base south of Dong Ha.

While Ed was in the hospital at Phu Bai, he learned that one of the Marines who had come up to Dong Ha in March to help us secure the site had been killed. Another Marine from his platoon, Kilo Company, Third Battalion/Fourth Marines told Ed that Corporal Douglas, with whom Ed had become good friends at Dong Ha, was shot by a sniper as he was attempting to go to the aid of a fellow wounded Marine. Ed said that sounded just like something "Doug" would do.

Cheri was med-evacced to Japan, then the Philippines, and eventually to St. Alban's Naval Hospital in Jamaica, NY. Ed mentioned that the further away from Vietnam, the worse the treatment got. He spent four months in the hospital where he had two skin grafts on his leg and his right eardrum was replaced. However, his accident in the minefield at Dong Ha and his injuries didn't stop Ed. He did two more tours in Vietnam.

In 1968, Cheri volunteered to go back to Vietnam, where he spent eighteen months at Pleiku Air Base in the Central Highlands. In January 1971, he went back to Vietnam for his third tour. He was at Phan Rang Air Base for thirty days, and then was reassigned to Cam Ranh Bay Air Base. He was assigned to the heavy weapons section with the 12th Security Police Squadron; however, Ed had to be med-evacced out of CRB to the Philadelphia Naval Hospital. He spent another three months in the hospital due to complications in his eardrum related to his injury in the minefield at Dong Ha.

Ed left the Air Force; however, he later joined the Army National Guard. He was a loader on an M-61 tank, then served in the Military Police, and later was assigned to an infantry unit. He retired from the Active Guard Reserve as a Staff Sergeant (E-6).

While Ed has never said anything, many of us believe that he should have been awarded the Purple Heart for his wounds. I guess the Air Force viewed the incident as an accident rather than an act of war by the enemy. However, Ed was severely wounded while performing a dangerous combat-related mission; one that he volunteered for, and one that was above and beyond the call of duty. If Cheri had stepped on a landmine while on routine patrol, he would most certainly have been awarded the Purple Heart. Similarly, Bob Stemock should have received the Airman's Medal[6] for clearing a path in the minefield to get Ed out. In the eyes of the Bandits, both Ed and Bob are heroes. I am sure that Ed and Bob would say they were simply doing their job.

Bob Stemock was the last Bandit to leave Dong Ha, in October 1966. He returned to Vietnam for a second tour in January 1968, just before the TET Offensive. He was assigned to the 623rd Air Police Squadron at Binh Thuy Air Base where he became the NCOIC of the Intelligence Unit. For his meritorious service at Binh Thuy, Bob was awarded the Bronze Star.[7]

Jack Case had joined the Air Force in 1955, a few days after his 17th birthday. A1C Case was on his second tour in Vietnam when he went with us to Dong Ha. Jack had been wounded at Bien Hoa Air Base in 1964. In 1965, he underwent Air Commando training at Forbes AFB, Kansas. He was assigned to the 4th Air Commando Squadron and sent back to Vietnam. He was reassigned to the 6250th Air Police Squadron and volunteered to go up to Dong Ha.

Case left the Air Force and joined the Army in 1969. He completed Ranger School at Fort Benning, Georgia, was assigned to Company K, 75th Rangers, and was sent back to Vietnam. All told, Jack served three tours in Vietnam and

---

[6] The Airman's Medal is awarded for heroism not involving actual combat with an armed enemy of the United States.

[7] The Bronze Star is awarded for meritorious service in connection to operations against an apposing armed force.

received four battle stars, including one that he had received at Dong Ha.

Jack was stationed at a base camp near Pleiku, in the Central Highlands. Ironically, his buddy at Dong Ha, Ed Cheri, was at Pleiku Air Base at about that same time. Apparently, neither one of them knew that the other was there.

Jack Case and Ed Cheri

While on a reconnaissance patrol, Jack stated that his Ranger unit came under heavy enemy fire, lasting for days, until they ran out of ammo and food.[8] During the battle, the North Vietnamese soldiers captured Jack, and he spent nineteen months as a prisoner of war. During his captivity, he was blindfolded, his arms tied to a stick behind his back. He was held in a small cage, fed only rice, and he was moved constantly from one camp to another. At one point, Case stated that he believed he was located in a village just above the DMZ in North Vietnam—close enough that he could hear and feel the ground tremble from the bombs being dropped in the DMZ.

U.S. Army Special Forces (Green Berets) raided the camp where Jack was being held, freeing him and twenty-two other American

---

[8] Personal communication with Jack Case on August 16, 2004.

POWs.[9] He was shipped back to the States where he ended up spending nine months at Walter Reed Army Medical Center in Washington, D.C. He was discharged from the Army in 1973.

Along with unit and campaign awards, Case received the Bronze Star with "V" device, the Purple Heart, the Prisoner of War Medal, and both the Air Force Commendation Medal and Army Commendation Medal. He also received the Parachute Basic ID Badge, Ranger Tab, and Combat Infantryman's Badge while serving in the U.S. Army.[10]

---

[9] *Ibid*, Jack Case.
[10] *Ibid,* Jack Case.

Our Replacements

Air police reinforcements began arriving at Dong Ha in mid-February and March, however, our total strength was only about twenty-five men. Packer was one of those replacements. I do not remember the names of the other new guys, but Mike Post, a kid from Utica, NY was among that group. One of the things you do remember about people is where they are from. Mike and I used to talk about home and got to be very good friends. I never really got to know the other replacements, however Sergeant Bradford remembered A2C Haney. He was one of the replacements that had come up to Dong Ha in February. Perhaps the close-knit relations among the Bandits may have prevented us from getting to know the others. I guess that is the way it is in war—you tend to be closer to those that have gone through the same things you have experienced.

It is impossible to chronicle all of the events that took place during our tour. We went out on post every night not knowing what would happen—if that night would bring the dreaded all-out attack. We had all volunteered for Dong Ha. We did not do it for medals or glory. It is hard to explain exactly why we did it. Certainly, we could have stayed at Tan Son Nhut where it was relatively safe. I think all of us wanted to see some action, but that wasn't the only reason. I think it was because we took pride in doing our part in the war. No one was eager to kill or to be killed. We were cops and it was our job to protect and to serve. To that end, we can proudly say that while we were at Dong Ha, we did our job with honor and distinction.

Sergeant Bradford, Jack Case, Ed Cheri, Bob Stemock, Dave Black, and John Bertolet were awarded the Air Force Commendation Medal[1] for their service at Dong Ha. Those who received the medal deserved it! Every man there should have received at least the AFCM—the point is that we all deserved it.

---

[1] The Air Force Commendation Medal is awarded for meritorious achievement or service.

I don't know if it was because we were Air Police assigned to a radar unit, or if we just slipped through the cracks and the paperwork was either not completed or simply lost. According to Bob Stemock, Major Cummings had stated that all airmen assigned to Dong Ha were to receive the AFCM. Since the medal was not presented until the individual recipient was assigned to his next duty station, we did not know that some received it while others did not. It was the farthest thing from our minds at the time. We all received battle stars on our Vietnam Service Medals.

Guys standing on the berm, circa June 1966

By the end of May, the original Bandits began to rotate back to the States. We had gone to Dong Ha as a group, but left one by one. Bob Stemock was the last Bandit to leave Dong Ha on September 30, 1966. John Bertolet, Jim Schneider, and myself left Dong Ha in the middle of June. Bert, reflecting upon his leaving, said:

> It had been a long hard pull and I was ready to go home. I am
> not sure what date I left Dong Ha but it was just a few days
> after A2C Joseph Packer was killed. Joe was an Air
> Policeman who had come up to Dong Ha in March.
> However, I know I was in Da Nang by June 20th because I
> sent a postcard home on that date.[2]

---

[2] Bertolet, John A. "Letters Home from Vietnam," *Tiger Flight, 13* (4), 2004, pp. 37-41.

According to Bertolet, we had a Port Call (the day you leave Vietnam) of July 3, 1966. We left Dong Ha sometime after June 16th (the day Packer was killed). Jim Schneider said:

> We were at Da Nang for a couple of weeks. While waiting for orders to Tan Son Nhut, we enjoyed going to China Beach during the day and watching a movie at the base theatre at night. We didn't have any recreational facilities, or the time to enjoy them if we had had them, at Dong Ha and it was nice to just sit back and relax for a while.[3]

When we finally arrived at TSN, there was some sort of mix up about our departure date. We had supposedly been booked on a flight to the U.S. on July 3, but we had been bumped off the list for some reason. We talked with an Air Force Colonel and our names were put back on the list. I vividly recall that I arrived home on July 4th and assume that John and Jim did also.

On the flight out of Saigon on our way home, I recalled that we stopped in Tokyo but I did not remember why. Jim Schneider was able to shed some light on this:

> We flew out on a Pan Am flight. However, during the flight, one of the passengers had a heart attack and our plane was diverted to Japan. A sergeant was taken off the plane and rushed to the hospital. I never knew what happened to him; whether he made it or not. We were on the ground for about an hour. We were not allowed off the plane during the layover. Our plane then took off headed for Travis AFB, CA, about sixty miles from San Francisco. From there, the three of us took off in different directions, Bill went to North Carolina and Bert went to Illinois. I flew to New York for a two-week leave at home before having to report in to my new assignment.[4]

---

[3] Personal communication with Jim Schneider on March 11, 2004.
[4] *Ibid*, Jim Schneider.

Our leader, TSgt. Bradford, continued his career in the Air Force, eventually retiring at the rank of Master Sergeant. Bob Stemock was promoted to Staff Sergeant while he was at Dong Ha. He returned to Vietnam for a second tour and then later cross-trained into Command Control. Bob became a crewmember aboard the "Looking Glass."[5] He retired as a Master Sergeant after twenty-two years of service. Doc Grover also retired as a Master Sergeant after twenty years of service. Subsequent to Dong Ha, Jack Case was assigned to Fort Fisher Air Station, North Carolina; however, he left the Air Force, joined the Army, and went back to Vietnam for a third tour. Jack was captured by the Viet Cong and spent nineteen months in a POW camp. Ed Cheri was med-evacced out of Dong Ha on September 11, 1966, however he would return to serve two more tours in Vietnam. Dave Black and Dave Green were discharged after their Vietnam tour and the rest of us returned to the States to serve out our four-year enlistments. Because of our Vietnam service, most of us got our first or second base of choice for reassignment—usually close to home.

Joe Lee was assigned to an Air Force detachment at the Wilmington, North Carolina airport. That was my home, but I didn't know about the detachment at the airport or I would have put in for it as my first choice. After I got home, I recall seeing Joe, and I remember that the two us went to Fort Fisher to see Jack. After that summer, we just lost contact with each other and were not reunited until the first reunion.

After completing his tour at Dong Ha, John Bertolet was assigned in August 1966, to the 87th Fighter Interceptor Squadron at Clinton County AFB, in Wilmington, Ohio. Jim Schneider went to the 4603rd Air Base Group, Stewart Air Force Base, New York.

I was fortunate to be assigned to law enforcement with the 354th Air Police Squadron at Myrtle Beach, AFB, South Carolina in August 1966 for my last nine and a half months—quite a contrast to the war and the austere living conditions at Dong Ha.

---

[5] "Looking Glass" was the U.S. Air Force codename for the EC-135 airborne command and control post in the sky. During the Cold War, the Strategic Air Command (SAC), headquartered at Offutt AFB in Nebraska, kept at least one EC-135 in the air at all times. Looking Glass had the capability of directing bombers and missiles from the air, should Offutt be destroyed by a nuclear attack.

We had our own firing range at Dong Ha and routinely fired all the weapons in our arsenal. Ironically, I was not allowed to carry a weapon other than a baton (nightstick) at Myrtle Beach until I re-qualified with the M-16 and pistol. In those days, Air Policemen wore "white hats," tan uniforms in the summer, dress blues in the winter, had a badge (Air Police shield), and carried 38s (38 cal. pistols). However, the duty of a gate guard could be kind of boring, especially after the excitement of Vietnam. I did a brief stint on the gates and then was assigned to law enforcement patrol. Having served three years in security (one year as a grunt in Vietnam), it was kind of nice finally to be a policeman. Nonetheless, I left the Air Force and never looked back.

While most of the Bandits were safe and sound at home, Ed Cheri and Bob Stemock were still at Dong Ha. There were about twenty-five air policemen assigned to the site and Ed and Bob were the "old" guys. They had been at Dong Ha when we lived in tents and ate C-rations. The tents were replaced with wooden huts and now air police were actually getting to sleep in them. They were working in shifts, whereas we had worked 24/7. We never had time to enjoy what little recreation there was at Dong Ha because we were always on the berm at night. The new unit even had an armory; however, I had liked the idea of keeping our weapons with us. We never knew when we would need them. Now, when the base came under attack, air police would have to go to the armory to check out weapons. With all these changes, Dong Ha was being transformed into a "regular" Air Force base. I liked it when we were a little outpost and we didn't have to worry about all those regulations.

In addition to their base defense duties, Air Police were now providing law enforcement patrols in Dong Ha. The nature of these patrols was to provide a U.S. military police presence in the village. Air Police also continued to provide armed escorts for convoys to Quang Tri and back.

Sam Baldon in Quang Tri City

Air Police continued to work long hours but there were moments when they could relax and enjoy a beer or a Coke with their buddies. The tents we lived in were gradually being replaced with new wooden huts. Though the tents were becoming a thing of the past and living conditions were improving; it was still rather austere.

I remember that some time after I got home from Vietnam I called Sergeant Bradford. I was on duty in the Air Police Office at Myrtle Beach AFB and on a whim decided to call the APO at Maxwell AFB, Alabama, hoping to locate Sarge. I do not remember if he answered the phone, but I was able to talk to him right away. I am not sure when this was, but it had to have been after September 11, 1966. That was the day Ed Cheri was blown up by a mine in the minefield at Dong Ha. The following is Sarge's recollection of that call:

> After Vietnam, I was assigned to the 3800th Security Police Squadron at Maxwell AFB, Alabama. I was safe but I worried about my troops that were still at Dong Ha. I received a telephone call at Maxwell from one of my troops after he got back from Vietnam. It was Bill Bland. He was

stationed at Myrtle Beach AFB, SC. I am not sure who told me, but later I heard that Ed Cheri had been seriously wounded by a land mine at Dong Ha. That was heart-breaking news, but Ed survived and we are good friends to this day.[6]

Four air policemen were assigned to Dong Ha in February 1966 and another eight or nine cops came up to Dong Ha in the middle of March 1966. Some of those troops might still have been there when Terry Sandman and twenty-nine others from the 366th Air Police Squadron at Da Nang were assigned (TDY) to Dong Ha in November 1966.

Unidentified AP and Mike Post on the main gate

[6] Bradford, Carl L. "A Message to My troops: Defenders of Dong Ha Air Base, Republic of Vietnam, 1965-1966." *Tiger Flight, 13,* (3), 2004, pp. 37-41.

And the War Went On

Terry Sandman arrived in Vietnam on July 28, 1966. Like the Bandits that preceded him at Dong Ha, he and several other Air Policemen volunteered to leave Da Nang and go up north to a place no one knew much about.

In the passage below, Terry describes the conditions of the bunkers that the Bandits had built to defend the site:

> The rainy season was ending. However, the perimeter defense bunker where I was assigned, located in the northeast corner of the air base had standing water in it from the leaking roof. Most of the perimeter bunkers manned by the Air Police were in need of repair or replacement. The troops assigned to them scrounged for plywood, canvas, and anything else we could find to build protection from the elements. The Monsoon had been especially hard on the sandbag bunkers and they had to be rebuilt.[1]

The bunker numbers may not mean much to the Bandits or to the readers, but you can get an idea of their location by Terry's description:

> Perimeter defense bunkers were located on the northwest corner (#5), about midway along the north berm (#10), on the northeast corner (#16), about midway along the east berm (#23), on the southeast corner (#31) and about midway on the south perimeter (#35). The main gate entry post was located about midway on the west side of the compound.[2]

---

[1] Personal communication with Terry Sandman on February 22, 2004.

[2] *Ibid*, Terry Sandman.

Terry Sandman, Da Nang Air Base

Bunker #31 was located on the southeast corner. In 1965-1966, this bunker was a 50 cal. machine gun position manned by Jack Case and Ed Cheri. Jack and Ed built this bunker and practically lived in it in1966. However, by now it was showing signs of deterioration.

Bunker #31 on the southeast corner

Bunker #5 was located on the northwest corner. I remember manning this bunker, at that time a 50 cal. machine gun position, with Mike Post, one of the replacements that came up to Dong Ha in March 1966. The minefield had been extended around the entire base perimeter.

Bunker #5 on the northwest corner

By the time Terry got to Dong Ha, the 50 cal. machine guns were gone. No one seems to know what happened to them. Bob Stemock, the last Bandit to leave Dong Ha on September 30, 1966 said that a 50 cal. was still positioned on the southeast corner of the site; however, he wasn't sure about the other 50 cal. positions.[3] All of the defensive bunkers were now M-60 posts. A second entry and exit gate was located on the northeast corner (Bunker #16). There was a dirt road that led into the village. I recall some Vietnamese huts being located just outside the perimeter. In fact, while the Bandits were at Dong Ha, we had our 50 cal. zeroed in on those huts.

Entry gate, Bunker 16 on the northeast corner

---

[3] Personal communication with Bob Stemock on March 2, 2004.

Air police were armed with M-16s, hand grenades, and the M-79 grenade launcher; however, now that they had an armory, air police had to turn in the M-60s, M-79, and ammunition at the end of each shift—though they were allowed to keep their M-16s on hand. An AP was assigned to the armory and was responsible for the maintenance and issuance of the weapons.

In the photo below, Terry and several of his buddies had just returned from a convoy to Quang Tri.

Terry Sandman, SSgt. Castellow, Don Cuddyer,
Richard Kordas, and Ed Way

Life at Dong Ha had been rough for the Bandits, but we enjoyed the freedom of being something of a renegade unit, without all the Air Force regulations, restrictions, and uniformity that were gradually creeping in during Terry's tour at Dong Ha. Terry was a "grunt" like us and he and his group of air policemen manned the same bunker positions and posts we had manned in defending the air base. While we had experienced several mortar attacks and small arms fire, the NVA were now pounding Dong Ha with rocket and artillery fire from positions located inside the DMZ.

The SAC "Sky Spot" radar site was not yet located at Dong Ha when most of the Bandits were there, with the possible exception of Bob Stemock and Ed Cheri. I know it wasn't there when I left in the middle of June 1966. Terry described the location of the Sky Spot radar site relative to the original "Waterboy" site:

The Sky Spot (SAC) radar site was located outside of the Air Force compound on the west side of the dirt road that ran from the airstrip and just north of the Marine's Delta Med. Sky Spot was about 100 feet by 100 feet in dimension and surrounded by steel revetments.[4]

Terry also described the build-up of NVA troops operating out of the DMZ in 1967:

Just a few miles to the north of Dong Ha was the Demilitarized Zone (DMZ), a buffer zone that divided North and South Vietnam. The DMZ was anything but demilitarized. The North Vietnamese Army had two divisions operating in and south of the DMZ. Supporting the two divisions were rocket units with 122mm and 140mm rockets. Over 100 artillery 130mm and 152mm guns were camouflaged and dug into the sides of hills in the DMZ where they could be rolled out to fire and then rolled back in for some protection against counter battery fire and aircraft bombs. Also, just north of the DMZ the North Vietnamese had Anti-Aircraft Artillery (AAA) and SAM SA-2 anti-aircraft missiles sites.[5]

What had begun as an isolated Air Force radar outpost defended by a small group of air policemen (Bandits) and approximately one hundred fifty airmen in 1965 was rapidly being transformed into a large Marine combat base. Terry reported:

By late 1966 and early 1967 it was quickly being engulfed by the much larger Marine combat base, which had been located there. The Air Force compound was located on the northeast perimeter of the combat base. Dong Ha was now part of

---

[4] Personal communication with Terry Sandman on February 22, 2004.
[5] *Ibid*, Terry Sandman.

Leatherneck Square, a quadrangle formed by the Marine combat bases at Con Thien and Gio Linh near the DMZ and Dong Ha and Cam Lo a few miles south. The Marines and NVA fought a series of bloody battles in this area as the NVA attempted to overrun Quang Tri Province.[6]

In early 1967, an element of the U.S. Army 1/44th Artillery Regiment was assigned to the air base. A Twin 40mm Tank "Duster" was placed on the east perimeter overlooking Highway 1. I wish we had had one of those at Dong Ha in 1965-1966.The Army also set up a Quad 50 cal. on top of an old concrete French bunker just north of the Sky Spot radar site. Previously, this post had been manned by Air Police from Terry's unit.

Near the end of Terry's six-month TDY assignment, he was permanently assigned to Dong Ha. The following is a list of Air Policemen that were assigned PCS[7] to Det. 1, 620th Tactical Control Squadron, Dong Ha Air Base in February 1967:

TSgt	Hilary V. Jones
SSgt	Eugene R. Castellow
SSgt	John T. VanDrunen
A1C	Phillip E. Gotschall
A1C	Robert J. Mueller
A1C	Jackie Osborn
A1C	Delma W. Ward
A1C	Calvin G. Watkins
A2C	John Boone
A2C	Emmet D. Brown
A2C	Harvey W. Caldwell
A2C	Donald W. Cuddyer
A2C	Robert Huertemantte
A2C	Richard V. Kordas
A2C	Kenneth Mainor
A2C	Roger L. McGuire
A2C	John J. Mitchell Jr.
A2C	Clent E. Rawlinson

[6] Ibid, Terry Sandman.
[7] Special Order A-1419 dated 24 February 1967 from Headquarters 366th Combat Support Group

A2C	John S. Rose
A2C	Terry G. Sandman
A2C	Richard T. Stein
A2C	James B. Teal
A2C	Clarence E. Way
A2C	Henry White Jr.
A2C	Raymond E. Wiler

The air base and the adjoining Marine combat base were hit with approximately forty rockets (140mm) on April 28, 1967. Three airmen were killed and an air policeman (Kenneth Mainor), who was manning the main gate, was wounded. An AC-47 (nicknamed "Spooky" by the Air Force) armed with electronic Gattling guns fired on the NVA positions, apparently with effect. The next day, according to Terry, a Marine patrol located the positions and found about fifty rockets. Terry added:

> The NVA had begun a major offensive with two divisions along the DMZ and northern Quang Tri Province. Their intent was to overrun the combat bases and eventually all of Quang Tri Province. All of the combat bases in Leatherneck Square were within range of the NVA rockets and artillery. The NVA also had the support of AAA and SAM missile anti aircraft fire.[8]

On May 18, 1967, 140mm rockets and 130mm artillery being fired by the NVA from the DMZ hit Dong Ha. Terry stated: "About 140 rocket, mortar and artillery rounds were fired by the NVA into the combat base, which included the Air Force, Marine and Navy areas. Fortunately, we had no KIA's on the air base; however, the Marines suffered a number of casualties."[9]

On July 3, 1967, NVA 130mm artillery rounds fired from the DMZ hit the air base, killing one airman and wounding several others. As a result, Terry stated the Sky Spot radar unit was eventually moved to a location south of Dong Ha, out of range of the NVA artillery.

---

[8] Personal communication with Terry Sandman on February 22, 2004.
[9] *Ibid*, Terry Sandman.

Just a few miles north of Dong Ha, Air Force B-52s and fighter-bombers constantly pounded the NVA troops, who were by this time freely operating out of the DMZ. Terry witnessed two fighter aircraft that had been downed by SAM missiles and reported that an O1-E "Bird-dog" spotter plane was blown out of the sky by a NVA missile fired from the DMZ. Terry added: "The B-52s hit the NVA positions both day and night. At Dong Ha, I felt the ground tremble from the impact of the bombs and at night I could see the flashes from the bombs ripple in the distance."[10]

On the ground, U.S. Marines bore the brunt of the fighting and suffered large casualties. The Marines had won the battles; however, on the home front, protest of the war was gaining momentum. The Air Force eventually pulled out of Dong Ha and later the Marine Corps abandoned its bases in the region.

With the withdrawal of American combat forces in Vietnam, the big offensive that we feared in 1966 finally occurred in 1972—what was called the Easter Offensive. The town of Quang Tri was destroyed and Dong Ha was overrun. In his book *The Bridge at Dong Ha* John Grider Miller described the heroics of Captain John Ripley (Col. USMC, Ret.) who placed demolitions under the bridge to blow it up, thus preventing the NVA tanks from crossing the Cua Viet River and entering the village of Dong Ha.[11]

South Vietnamese Marines, accompanied by U.S. Marine advisors, recaptured Quang Tri, but the war was over—though Saigon did not fall until 1975.

Air police had been in Vietnam since 1961 at the air bases located at Tan Son Nhut, Bien Hoa, and Da Nang. Staff Sergeant Terrance Jenson was the first air policeman to give his life in Vietnam on July 1, 1965 at Da Nang Air Base.[12] Sgt. Jenson and another air policeman encountered a sapper team that had made its way onto the flight line. Since this event occurred just days before I arrived in Vietnam, it stuck in my mind as I patrolled the flight line and perimeter of Tan Son Nhut Air Base. Before the war was over, one hundred eleven U.S. Air Force police, including A2C Joseph Packer at Dong Ha in 1966, were killed in

---

[10] *Ibid*, Terry Sandman.

[11] Miller, John G. *The Bridge at Dong Ha*. Annapolis, MD: Naval Institute Press, 1996.

[12] Air Force Security Police Association. *Air Force Security Police*. Paducah, KY: Turner Publishing, 1996, p. 32.

action or in the line of duty.[13] However, this number only represents those casualties that have been verified by the Vietnam Security Police Association. On January 31, 1968 during the TET Offensive, four security policemen with the 377th Security Police Squadron were killed at the 051 Gate at Tan Son Nhut Air Base. Most of us (Bandits) had manned that gate during our tour at TSN. Viet Cong attacked the air base, however in the battle that ensued, members of the 377th SPS inflicted large numbers of casualties on the enemy. Two more security policemen from the 3rd Security Police Squadron at Bien Hoa Air Base also were killed on that date.

The Paris Peace Accords in 1973 brought about the withdrawal of all U.S. forces in Vietnam. The last remaining Air Force operational unit in Vietnam, the 377th SPS, withdrew from Tan Son Nhut Air Base on March 29, 1973.[14] When the North Vietnamese Army rolled into Saigon in 1975, more than three hundred security policemen from the 3rd Security Police Group, stationed at Clark AB in the Philippines, were involved in the airlift operation that evacuated all remaining American personnel from Tan Son Nhut Air Base on April 29th and 30th.[15] C-141s flew during the day and C-130s flew in at night. The last C-130 into TSN was hit by NVA rockets and exploded on the runway in the early morning hours of April 30th. Rockets bombarded the base all through the night. In addition, security police fought off an elite South Vietnamese paratrooper unit that attempted to board the last C-141 out of Vietnam. The last ten security policemen boarded a CH-53 helicopter around 1830 (8:30 p.m.) on the 30th. They were the last American forces out of Vietnam.

The Vietnam War was over. However, on May 13, 1975, eighteen members of the 56th Security Police Squadron, Nhakon Phanom AB, Thailand, were killed in a helicopter crash while involved in the *SS Mayaguez* rescue operation in Cambodia.

For its service in the Vietnam War, the 620th Tactical Control Squadron received the following unit awards: Air Force Outstanding Unit Award with Combat "V" device and the RVN

[13] Vietnam Security Police Association (USAF). "Roll of Honor." Retrieved from http://www.vspa/memorial on July 25, 2005.
[14] AFSPA, *Air Force Security Police*, 1996, p. 35.
[15] *Ibid*, p. 35.

Gallantry Cross Unit Citation with Palm. The Air Force
Outstanding Unit Award w/V device[16] was issued under Special
Order GB-3, dated 5 January 1968 and was signed by J. P.
McConnell, General, USAF, Chief of Staff. There were several
inclusive dates for the award; however, the period between
September 1, 1965 and May 25, 1967 would correspond to the
time when we were at Dong Ha. Since the Bandits were assigned
to the 620th TCS, we all have that award, even though it is not
listed on our DD-214. In fact, most of us were discharged from
the Air Force before General McConnell signed the order in
1968. The Republic of Vietnam Gallantry Cross w/Palm was
awarded to the unit for the period between April 1, 1966 and
January 28, 1973; however, it is not listed on our DD-214 either.

---

[16] A bronze "V" on The Ribbon denotes combat service.

Our Legacy

The purpose of this chapter is to provide a brief account of our legacy to the U.S. Air Force police and security forces. Today's Air Force Security Forces members are highly trained, dedicated, and professional airmen. The SF motto is *Defensor Fortis* (Defenders of the Force). Security Forces members can be proud of the rich history and tradition of the Air/Security Police that preceded them. The story of Bradford's Bandits at Dong Ha Air Base, Vietnam in 1965-1966 is a small part of that heritage.

The Air Force police have witnessed three major name changes. First, from Military Police to Air Police when the Air Force separated from the Army Air Force (AAF) in 1948, secondly from Air Police to Security Police in 1966, and lastly from Security Police to Security Forces in 1997.[1]

Though the designation to Security Police was officially made in January 1966, we were not aware of the name change at Dong Ha. In fact, when I was discharged from the Air Force in June of 1967, I was still identified as an Air Policeman on my DD-214. During the Vietnam War, Air Police and Security Police guarded the air bases and radar sites from the DMZ to the Me Cong Delta from enemy attacks. We were the "grunts" of the Air Force and proud of it.

In Vietnam, Air Force AP/SPs were armed with 50 cal. and M-60 machine guns, 81mm mortars, hand grenades and M-79 grenade launchers as well as other heavy weapons. AP/SPs manned the machine gun bunkers and walked the line along the perimeter, often alone rather than in large units or strike forces. For those AP/SPs who were killed in the line of duty, it did not matter whether they were called Air Police or Security Police or that they were airmen rather than soldiers or Marines—they

---

[1] Bland, William D. "What's in a Name? Revisited: A Review from Military Police to Today's Security Forces." *Tiger Flight, 10* (5), 2001, pp. 7, 46.

were the "Defenders of the Force." They wore their shields as badges of courage.

In 1966, the Air Force developed Operation Safeside with the activation of the 1041st Security Strike Force. Security Police were trained at the U.S. Army Ranger School at Fort Benning, Georgia. The 1041st was assigned to Phu Cat, Vietnam in January 1967. The mission of the Strike Force was to defend air bases "outside the wire." Lessons learned from Phu Cat were soon incorporated into the training of all Security Police units in Vietnam.[2]

At Dong Ha in 1965-1966, Air Police were using small unit tactics to guard the air base "outside the wire" long before this became standard procedure in the Air Force. Two of our members, Jack Case and Bob Stemock, had received Air Commando training by the Army's elite Special Forces. We also went out on ambush details with U.S. Marines while they were at Dong Ha. At other air bases, Air Police volunteered to fly with Army helicopter crews as door gunners; however, most of these missions were "unofficial"—thus they were never recognized by the Air Force. These untold stories are a part of the legacy of today's Security Forces.

From Korea, to Vietnam, to the Gulf War, and in peacetime as well as during the Cold War, AP/SPs performed their duty with distinction and honor. In 1996, a truck loaded with explosives killed nineteen American airmen at the Khobar Towers in Saudi Arabia.[3] The quick reaction of Security Police personnel saved countless other lives. In the aftermath of the September 11th terrorist attacks on America, Air National Guard Security Forces members were called up to help provide security at our nation's airports.[4]

In the war on terrorism, members of the 455th Expeditionary Security Forces Squadron worked with the Army to secure Bagram Air Base, Afghanistan. They provided perimeter security, guarded entry control points, and patrolled outside the wire to

---

[2] Air Force Security Police Association. *Air Force Security Police*, Paducah, KY: Turner Publishing Company, 1996, p. 34.

[3] Bland, William D. "The New Terrorism." *Tiger Flight, 11* (5), 2002, pp. 39-41.

[4] Bland, William D. "Homeland Defense: The Military's New Mission in the War on Terror." *Tiger Flight, 11* (1), 2002, pp. 45-46.

protect the air base. During the height of the Iraq War, Air Force
Security Forces members jumped with the Army's 173rd
Airborne Brigade into northern Iraq. SFs from the 786th
Expeditionary Security Forces Squadron, parachuted into Bashur
Airfield, Iraq. Along with the airborne soldiers, SFs secured the
base, stood guard at entry control points and built defensive firing
positions.[5]

Though the name has changed several times, the history and
tradition of the Air Force police lives on today with the U.S. Air
Force Security Forces. SFs are continuing that tradition as
evidenced by their valiant performance in places like Afghanistan
and Iraq. The past was ours, but the present is theirs; we salute
them. They are making their own history to pass on to the future
generation of Air Force police/security forces. *Defensor Fortis.*

---

[5] Bland, William D. "Military Police: A Review of the Police and Security Forces of the U.S. Armed
Services." *Tiger Flight, 12* (6), 2003, pp. 37-39.

Agent Orange

Life at Dong Ha was dangerous in other ways, too. We went through several mortar attacks, firefights, harassing sniper rounds, exploding landmines, and the fear of an all-out attack. Nevertheless, the most hazardous assault on our persons, as it would turn out, was from the use of a chemical called Agent Orange.

Agent Orange, a chemical defoliant used in Vietnam, has been linked to a number of diseases, including Type II Diabetes. During our tour in Vietnam and especially at Dong Ha, we had all been exposed to this chemical. Air Force Ranch Hand crews, flying C-123s, used aerial spraying techniques to kill the jungle foliage around the Dong Ha Air Base. The chemical toxins (dioxin) in the Agent Orange got on our skin, in our water supply, and in the air we breathed. Though Agent Orange was used in all four military zones in Vietnam, it was most heavily used in the area around the demarcation zone.[1] Dong Ha was less than ten miles from the DMZ.

The name Agent Orange derives from the orange stripes on the 55-gallon drums used to store the chemical. Bob Stemock recalled mixing a chemical that he later found out was Agent Orange with diesel fuel to spray on the "no man's" area between the berm and the outer fence line. This was done in order to kill the vegetation that, if left uncontrolled, would pull the trip wire pins on the mines in the minefield.

Not until many years after the war did the government reveal that a number of diseases were linked to Agent Orange. Today, Bob Stemock has Type II Diabetes. In addition, Sergeant Bradford, John Bertolet, Dave Green, Doc Grover, and Jim Schneider have this disease. That is a ratio of 1:2 compared to the national average of 1:20. Since gathering this information, I have

---

[1] "Agent Orange: Information for Veterans Who Served in Vietnam." Washington, DC: Department of Veteran Affairs, 2003.

also been diagnosed with diabetes. However, I am not on any type of medication as of yet. With my diagnosis, that means that more than half of the Bandits have this disease. The rest of the Bandits may also have diabetes and don't know it, thus everyone who has not yet been diagnosed, needs to be tested. Another disease linked to Agent Orange is spina bifida. Sam Baldon experienced the loss of two infants, possibly linked to this birth defect. In 2005, Sergeant Bradford was also diagnosed with non-Hodgkin's lymphoma and Jim Schneider has neuropathy in his legs. Both of these diseases are included in a list of illnesses linked to Agent Orange.

In 1991, Congress passed the Agent Orange Act (Public Law 102-4).[2] The act established a process by which a number of illnesses are "presumed" to be due to herbicide exposure by Vietnam veterans. Based on the National Academy of Sciences (NAS) Institute of Medicine 1994 report, illnesses included:soft tissue sarcoma, non-Hodgkin's lymphoma, Hodgkin's disease, Chloracne, porphyria custanea tarda, multiple myeloma, and respiratory cancers.

In 1996, Vietnam veterans' children born with spina bifida also became eligible for compensation and other VA services. Based on 1996, 1998, 2000, and 2002 NAS reports, the VA added to the list: acute or subacute transient peripheral neuropathy, type II diabetes, prostate cancer, and chronic lymphocytic leukemia.

The Agent Orange Act of 1991 defined "presumptive exposure" as giving the benefit of the doubt to the veteran, by presuming that a Vietnam veteran diagnosed with one or more of these illnesses acquired them through Agent Orange exposure. As a result, Vietnam veterans can file claims for disability compensation. Disability, however, is not automatic; a veteran must file a claim with the Veterans Administration. Vietnam veterans should contact the nearest VA medical center to schedule an Agent Orange Registry examination. This exam provides an entrance into the VA health system; however, it does not constitute a claim for compensation from the VA. If diagnosed with an Agent Orange illness, the veteran can then file a claim with the VA.

---

[2] "NAS Agent Orange Update 2004." *Agent Orange Review*. Washington, DC: Department of Veteran Affairs, April 2005.

Epilogue

The years went by but I never forgot the Bandits. Each one was an individual with his own unique personality but together we were Bandits. The war brought us together but it was the bond we shared at Dong Ha that unites us today. The story did not end here for this group of Vietnam veterans. It took thirty-six years, but we located all eleven Bandits and reunited with one another. It is a story in itself how we found everyone. Once we did, there was never any doubt that we would all get back together again.

It was quite common in the military to call each other by one's last name, or a nickname, rather than by a first name. In Vietnam, we called Bertolet by his nickname "Bert." I was able to find his name listed on a Vietnam veteran's website. The only information provided was name, rank, military specialty, and branch of service.

In the Air Force, military specialty is referred to as Air Force Specialty Code or AFSC. For example, the code for Air Police was 77150 or 77170 (Air Police Supervisor). John should have been listed as a 77150, however his AFSC was listed as 99014 (authorized airman, unspecified). Since I had found my name on this website and was also listed as 99014, I was pretty sure this was the right Bertolet. In addition, A2C Joseph Packer was listed as 99014. The only explanation that I can think of for the discrepancy in the AFSC is that possibly that was how we were listed in the Det. 1, 620th TCS Table of Organization.

I did not remember where Bert was from, so I did a national telephone search online and came up with a number of listings for John Bertolet. By the way, finding Bertolet was easier than trying to find someone named Green or Black. The second name on the list was John A. Bertolet. I called that number and John answered. The following is Bert's recollection of the conversation:

How did this all get started? For me, it started with a phone call on Sunday, January 20, 2002. Thoughts of Vietnam,

Saigon, Tan Son Nhut, Dong Ha and the ten other original Bandits that I served with were just not on my mind. Then the phone rang. When I answered, the unfamiliar voice on the other end asked, "Is this John Bertolet (pronouncing it Bert-o-lay)?" I answered, "Yes." "Are you a Vietnam veteran?" the caller questioned. I said, "Yes, I am." He then asked, "Were you in the Air Police in Vietnam?" Again I said, "I was." Then the caller continued, "Were you in Dong Ha?" I again answered, "Yes."

The next question was, "Do you remember Bill Bland?" I said, "Yes I do!" I sure did remember that name. He then said, "You're talking to him!"

Needless to say, we talked for about two hours that Sunday. It was great to talk to Bill again. He and I had shared many nights working together in a sandbag bunker at Dong Ha. It had been more than thirty-five years since we had spoken. We were very close comrades, friends, Bunker buddies, and most of all Bandits.

For me that call began the process of wanting to find the eleven original Air Policemen who became known as Bradford's Bandits. I became rather obsessed in looking for all of the Vietnam memorabilia that I still had. I thought that I had lots, but after searching everywhere, discovered I had very little.[1]

Nevertheless, John had kept a copy of the orders sending us up to Dong Ha. That was key, because it had the first names and middle initials for each of the Bandits. In Vietnam, we would not have called Sergeant Bradford by his first name; it would have been Tech Sergeant, Sergeant, or Sarge. I remembered however that Sarge was from Alabama. I had called him at Maxwell AFB,

---

[1] Personal communication with John Bertolet on July 21, 2002.

Alabama soon after I had returned home from Vietnam in 1966. Now that I had his first name, I was able find him the very next night.

I found a number listed for a Carl L. Bradford located in New Market, Alabama. I called that number and a woman (his wife, Elizabeth) answered. I asked for Sergeant Bradford and she said he was not home. I still wasn't sure that I had contacted the right person so I asked her if her husband was an Air Force sergeant; she said "yes." I told her my name and said I was a member of the Bradford Bandits. She knew about the Bandits. Elizabeth said she would have Carl call me when he got home. About thirty minutes later, the phone rang and it was Sarge.

It just sort of boomeranged from there. Sarge called Bob Stemock later that night. Bob had Ed Cheri's telephone number. And by the next day, Sarge had also located Jack Case. John Bertolet, Jim Schneider, and myself had come home from Vietnam together and John had kept a copy of Jim's orders, which listed his home address while on leave. Sometime, later that week, Bert found Jim in New York. I knew that Joe Lee was from a small town outside of Raleigh, NC and in about four or five telephone calls, I was able to find him. Thus, within the span of about ten days, we had found eight of the original Bandits.

Only three more Bandits to go; however it would take several months to find Black, Green, and Baldon. Sarge wrote letters to the Veteran's Administration (VA) and even to the Governor of Ohio (that's how he found Dave Black). Next, Sarge got a call from Dave Green, followed about a month later by a call from Sam Baldon. Sarge called me about six o'clock on a Saturday morning. He was really excited over finding Sam and couldn't wait to let everyone know. That was Sarge for you; he cared about each one of his Bandits and wasn't going to be satisfied until he found them all.

We planned a reunion in Myrtle Beach, SC for July 18 through July 22, 2002. All eleven members were present. Bandits, their wives, and other family members from as far away as California and Oregon, Illinois, New York, Pennsylvania, Florida, Alabama and nearby North and South Carolina converged on the beach resort.

We were welcomed by the local CBS affiliate (WBTW), Channel 13, who aired our reunion story on July 19th. We stayed at the Holiday Inn SunSpree in Surfside Beach. The local VFW (Post 10420) in Murrells Inlet, SC provided space for our formal meeting on July 20th. We enjoyed the sun and the beach, but most of all we bonded together as we had thirty-seven years earlier in 1965. Wives who may have come along just to please their husbands soon bonded as if they had known each other for years.

This reunion would never have happened if not for the bond we all shared at Dong Ha, and especially the devotion and loyalty we all had for our leader, Sergeant Bradford. He had earned our respect by "taking care of his troops" during the war. It was his leadership and our commitment to one another that had gotten us through the war. The highest tribute to Sergeant Bradford is that more than thirty-six years later, we were still his Bandits.

Our experience in Vietnam had forever transformed our lives. Most of us were only twenty or twenty-one when we served in Vietnam. Now, in our late fifties and early sixties, all are living successful lives. Yet, none of us had forgotten our time together as "Bandits." Although we had not seen each other for all those years, we closed the circle and finally came home from the war as a group. The Vietnam War has long since been over, but old friendships were renewed and new friendships were made with family members of the Bandits. It is difficult to put into words what this reunion meant to us, both individually and collectively. The best way I know how to say it is that we were "soldiers" and now we are brothers.

The term soldier was used in the above passage in the general context of warrior or combatant. We were airmen and are proud of our military service in the U.S. Air Force. As air police, we were the boots on the ground that protected Air Force personnel and installations.

John Bertolet said:

> After the reunion in Myrtle Beach in July 2002, I came to the realization that our meeting was a special moment in my life.

For the first time I could sit down and talk about the Vietnam War in a way that I had never been able to do before. It was with men who understood, men who were there and shared the experiences with me. It was a thrilling day for me to be face-to-face once again with the men who had been my buddies during the war. We had all gone our separate ways after Vietnam, but now we are best of friends.[2]

In one of our many telephone conversations prior to the reunion, I learned that Sarge was an Alabama football fan. Also, in the summer of 2002, before our reunion, a television movie called The Junction Boys aired, and it was about (the legendary Alabama coach) Paul "Bear" Bryant's first season at Texas A & M University. That team went one and nine. However, Coach Bryant and his players were reunited many years later, much like Sergeant Bradford was with his Bandits at our reunion.

The following year, July 13-17, 2003, we held our second reunion in Branson, Missouri. We invited two new people to this reunion. One was William "Doc" Grover, the medic at Dong Ha who had treated our mascot Bandit for wounds suffered from a landmine explosion. The other invitee was Terry Sandman, an Air Policeman who served at Dong Ha from 1966-1967. Terry was a grunt like us; he manned the same posts, and he and his fellow air policemen defended Dong Ha, just as we had done. Doc and Terry were unanimously voted Honorary Bandits and are now a part of our Bandit family.

Almost forty years after our service in Vietnam, all of the Bandits are doing well. Carl Bradford retired from the U.S. Air Force as a Master Sergeant and he and his wife Elizabeth live in New Market, Alabama. Bob Stemock retired from the U.S. Air Force at the rank of Master Sergeant. He then worked for fourteen years as a deputy sheriff and corrections officer in Orange County, Florida. Bob and his wife Jan live in Apopka, Florida. Bill "Doc" Grover also retired from the U.S. Air Force as a Master Sergeant. After his retirement, he worked in civilian law enforcement for a couple of years as a deputy sheriff in Chilton County, Alabama. Doc and his wife Minnie live in Jones, Alabama.

---

[2] Personal communication with John Bertolet on July 25, 2002.

Jack Case retired from the U.S. Army as a Staff Sergeant. He is currently Command Sergeant Major in the South Carolina State Guard. Jack's beloved wife Ruby passed away shortly after our first reunion in 2002. Jack lives in New Ellenton, South Carolina. Ed Cheri retired from the Army Active Guard and is currently a Sergeant in the Montgomery County Sheriff's Department (Pennsylvania), where he is commander of the bomb disposal unit. He credits Jack Case and Bob Stemock with first introducing him to explosives at Dong Ha. Ed and his wife Sheila live in King of Prussia, Pennsylvania. Sam Baldon is a Lieutenant with the Los Angeles County Fire Department. He and his wife Carol reside in Azusa, California.

After leaving the service, Dave Green attended Oregon State University. He also worked as a police officer in Corvallis, Oregon. Dave received a bachelor's degree in elementary education from Portland State University. He also holds a teaching certificate in reading. He was a fourth grade teacher until his retirement in 2004. Dave and his wife Nancy live in Portland, Oregon. Joe Lee is an electrician. He works for North Carolina State University in Raleigh, North Carolina. Joe and his wife Gloria live in Angier, North Carolina.

John Bertolet is a manager for a manufacturing company and he and his wife Vicki live in Mattoon, Illinois. Dave Black is a successful businessman and he and his wife Martha reside in Daytona Beach, Florida. Jim Schneider is a supervisor in a manufacturing plant. Jim and his wife Fran live in Washingtonville, New York. Terry Sandman retired as a Lieutenant after serving twenty-two years with the U.S. Secret Service (Uniformed Division) in Washington, DC. Terry and his wife Debbie presently reside in Oak Grove, Missouri.

Upon completing my four-year enlistment in the Air Force, I went to college on the G. I. Bill. I earned a Bachelor of Arts in Social Science with concentrations in Psychology and Political Science from the University of North Carolina at Wilmington, a Master of Arts in Psychology from Appalachian State University, and a Master of Sociology and a Doctor of Philosophy in Sociology with specialization in Social Psychology from North Carolina State University.

Earlier in my career, I worked as a vocational rehabilitation counselor and staff psychologist. From 1975 to 2005, I held academic appointments in Psychology, Sociology, and Criminology at a number of colleges and universities. Currently, I am living in my hometown of Wilmington, North Carolina.

Our third reunion was held July 11-15, 2004, once again at the Holiday Inn SunSpree Resort located in Surfside Beach, SC.

We had our fourth reunion July 10-14, 2005. This was a special reunion because it was held in Huntsville, Alabama, only a few miles from Sarge's home in New Market. It was indeed a real pleasure for all the Bandits to meet Sarge's family and his considerably large extended family. Sarge is truly blessed to have such a wonderful family.

We had our formal meeting at the local VFW (Post 2702) on July 12th. Sarge is a Lifetime Member of Post 2702. The main point that should be emphasized here is that the real Bandit story is about family. It is not a military story or a war story per se—it is a story about the bond we shared in Vietnam during the war nearly forty years ago that we have been fortunate enough to preserve to the present day.

Our reunions are unique among military reunions in that we are an intact unit that served together at the same time and place. My wish is that some day we might be able to locate some of the other air policemen that served with us at Dong Ha.

Recently, I came across a poem written by David Green entitled "Bradford's Bandits." It was located in a stack of other material from our first reunion. In writing this book, I have attempted to describe our story; however, Dave has a creative talent for words that get right to the heart of the matter. He wrote this poem about a week before our first reunion in Myrtle Beach, South Carolina.

BRADFORD'S BANDITS

In the year of nineteen sixty-five,
At Tan Son Nhut, when we were young...
We volunteered (being brash and dumb),
Not knowing then what we'd become.

By the year of nineteen sixty-six,
Above Quang Tri, near the DMZ,
In a little town they called Dong Ha,
We quickly learned that we would be:

BRADFORD'S BANDITS, THEN!
BRADFORD'S BANDITS, NOW!
A Brotherhood of ten young men,
Grew strong, as one, somehow.

The time that's past has been a gift,
Gave by men who heard the call.
Gave by men who gave their all...
Their names are carved upon The Wall.

Ten different pathways led us here
To this last guardmount where we each
Salute the Sarge who calls the roll
On the salty sand of Myrtle Beach.

BRADFORD'S BANDITS, NOW!
BRADFORD'S BANDITS, THEN!
This Brotherhood of ten, somehow,
United once again.

The knife of time etched us deep,
It's carved its lines on brow and cheek.
When time no more can life replace
I hope to hear in that Fair-Place:

BRADFORD'S BANDITS, ALL!
BANDITS TO THE END!
YOUR NAMES ARE ENTERED ON THE WALL
OF GRACE. PLEASE MARCH RIGHT IN.[3]

We were not heroes, but we served with heroes. During the Vietnam War (1964-1975), a total of 8,744,000 U.S. servicemen

---

[3] Green, David M. "Bradford's Bandits," Unpublished poem, July 8, 2002.

and women served worldwide. Out of that number, 3,403,000 American service members served in Southeast Asia.[4] There were a total of 58,209 deaths including 47,424 battle deaths and 10,785 other deaths (in-theater). Additional casualties included 153,303 non-mortal woundings. They are the true heroes of the war.

During the Bandit's tour of duty, we had only nine deaths (seven killed in action and two deaths in the line of duty) and one non-mortal wounding. They are our heroes. We also have at least seven members of our group who developed Type II diabetes as well as other diseases linked to exposure to Agent Orange in Vietnam. We were very fortunate to survive Vietnam and to have lived relatively long successful lives; however, at the time of this writing, at least five of our members are seriously ill or in poor health. We were able to locate all of the original eleven Bandits and to have at least one reunion in which everyone was present. Later, we were able to find Doc Grover and Terry Sandman. We are brothers.

I think Jim Schneider summed up the feelings that many of the Bandits had after that first reunion. Jim said:

> Until the first Bandit reunion in Myrtle Beach, I had forgotten about the war. It was just not something that I talked about, not even with my wife. I don't consider myself a hero, but I was proud to have served my country, especially with the Bandits. We did our duty and I feel good about that, but the war seems like a long time ago for me. However, my wife Fran and I enjoy the close association we have with the other Bandits and their families today.[5]

The reunions are an opportunity for a bunch of guys to reminisce about the war, but more importantly, they are a celebration of life. We came home, many did not. Though some Bandits are Democrats and others are Republicans, some are liberal and others are conservative, we are all Americans who are proud of our service to our country and the time we spent together in a war no one wanted to remember.

---

[4] "America's Wars." Washington, DC: Department of Veterans Affairs, September 2005.
[5] Personal communication with Jim Schneider on July 21, 2002.

Photo Credits

Front cover (Jack Case, David Black, and Bandit), U.S. Air Force photo

Page v (Tech. Sergeant Bradford, Dong Ha, 1966), John Bertolet photo

Page 4 (A2C Bland, 6250th APS, 1965), Author's photo

Page 5 (John Bertolet, Tan Son Nhut, 1965), John Bertolet photo

Page 10 (Bob Hope, Tan Son Nhut, 1965), John Bertolet photo

Page 11 (Bob Hope Show, Tan Son Nhut, 1965), Sam Baldon photo

Page 11 (My Canh Restaurant, 1965), Jim Schneider photo

Page 12 (Hotel bombing in Saigon, 1965), John Bertolet photo

Page 16 (Jim Schneider, David Green, and John Bertolet), David Green photo

Page 17 (Claymore mine), David Green photo

Page 18 (View of the east perimeter), David Green photo

Page 19 (Back view of the 50 cal. bunker on the southeast corner), Ed Cheri photo

Page 20 (Joe Lee and John Bertolet), David Green photo

Page 21 (Bill Bland cleaning his weapon), David Green photo

Page 22 (Dave Green, 50 cal. located on the northeast corner), David Green photo

Page 26 (View of the south berm), Sam Baldon photo

Page 27 (Unexploded mortar round), David Green photo

Page 30 (Rifle bunker on the south berm), Sam Baldon photo

Page 35 (ARVN 105mm Howitzer), John Bertolet photo

Page 36 (Col. Daniel and Lt. Col. Meyer inspecting 50 cal. machine gun post), U.S. Air Force photo

Page 39 (Mortar damage to mess hall), John Bertolet photo

Page 39 (Dave Black and Jack Case with little Vietnamese girl), U.S. Air Force photo

Page 43 (Sam Baldon providing personal security for Mr. Mitchum), Sam Baldon photo

Page 43 (Dave Green and unidentified Air Policeman), David Green photo

Page 46 (Jim Schneider), David Green photo

Page 47 (Bob Stemock surrounded by Vietnamese children), Sam Baldon photo

Page 49 (Little Vietnamese girl in the village of Dong Ha), Sam Baldon photo

Page 49 (Joe Lee and Vietnamese children), David Green photo

Page 50 (Airmen cleaning mess kits), Sam Baldon photo

Page 54 (Doc Grover, Sgt. Bradford, and Bandit), Sam Baldon photo

Page 56 (Ed Cheri, Sgt. Bradford, Sam Baldon, Jack Case, and Bandit), Sam Baldon photo

Page 57 (Jim Schneider and Bandit), Sam Baldon photo

Page 62 (Change of command), John Bertolet photo

Page 63 (Ed Cheri and Jack Case), David Green photo

Page 63 (TSgt. Bradford on the airstrip), David Green photo

Page 65 (Putting Sarge on the plane), David Green photo

Page 66 (Bandits on the end of the runway), David Green photo

Page 72 (Air Police Command Post), John Bertolet photo

Page 75 (Jack Case showing off some our weapons), David Green photo

Page 80 (Joseph Packer, unidentified AP, and Ed Cheri), Ed Cheri photo

Page 81 (Wrecked weapons carrier), Ed Cheri photo

Page 85 (Jack Case and Ed Cheri), Ed Cheri photo

Page 88 (Guys standing on the berm, circa June 1966), John Bertolet photo

Page 92 (Sam Baldon in Quang Tri City), Sam Baldon photo

Page 93 (Unidentified AP and Mike Post on the main gate), Ed Cheri photo

Page 96 (Terry Sandman, Da Nang Air Base), Terry Sandman photo

Page 96 (Bunker #31 on the southeast corner), Terry Sandman photo

Page 97 (Bunker #5 on the northwest corner), Terry Sandman photo

Page 97 (Entry gate, Bunker #16 on the northeast corner), Terry Sandman photo

Page 98 (Terry Sandman, SSgt. Castellow, Don Cuddyer, Richard Kordas, and Ed Way), Terry Sandman photo

Back cover (Tech. Sergeant Carl Bradford, Dong Ha, 1966), John Bertolet photo

Index

William D. Bland served in the United States Air Force from 1963 to 1967. He volunteered for Vietnam and served at the Tan Son Nhut Air Base. He later volunteered to serve at Dong Ha Air Base with the 620th Tactical Control Squadron. He holds a Ph.D. in Sociology and Masters degrees in Psychology and Sociology. He has taught Psychology, Sociology, and Criminology at several colleges and universities for over thirty years. Other books by Dr. Bland are *Aging Parents: Continuity and Change in Adult Life* (Cummings & Hathaway, 1998) and *Careers in Federal and Military Law Enforcement* (Cummings & Hathaway, 1999). He makes his home in Wilmington, North Carolina.